Ulcer
Crohn's Disease
Cookbook

Specific Carbohydrate Diet & Paleo

*Cookbook Featuring 170 Delicious
Easy Recipes*

By EMANUEL D'SOUSA

TABLE OF CONTENT

DESCRIPTION 8

INTRODUCTION TO THE PALEO DIET 9

INTRODUCTION TO THE SPECIFIC CARBOHYDRATE DIET 10

WHAT'S WRONG WITH THE MODERN DIET 11

WHY YOU SHOULD START ON THESE DIETS 12

BENEFITS OF THE SCD & PALEO DIET...................14

DO'S AND DON'TS 15

GROCERY LIST..17

PALEO RECIPES 21

1. HEAVENLY HAM N' EGGS 22
2. SUPPER VEGGIE OMELETTE 23
3. VEGGIE-BUN SANDWICH 24
4. TURKEY LOW CARB PALEO PATTIES..................................... 25
5. KALE BREAKFAST MUFFIN... 26
6. ALMOND FLOUR BLUEBERRY WAFFLES................................. 27
7. RASPBERRY-ALMOND PANCAKES 28
8. CUCUMBER SANDWICH 29
9. BERRY-COCONUT SHAKE.. 30
10. SOUTHERN-FRANCE STYLE SCRAMBLED EGGS 31
12. HASH-CAVEMAN STYLE BREAKFAST 33
13. PALEO STYLE GRANOLA BARS 35
14. APPLE-SPICEY MUFFINS 36
15. PALEO PUMPKIN MUFFINS 37

16. PALEO SAFE BEEF JERKY 39

17. PALEO HONEY BUTTER ROASTED WALNUTS SLOW COOKER RECIPE 40

18. MIXED SPICY NUTS 41

19. BANANA WITH COCONUT & ALMOND BUTTER 42

20. COCONUT WHIPPED CREAM 43

21. PALEO PIZZA 44

22. CASHEW BUTTER BANANA WRAP 45

23. SMOKED SALMON EGGS WRAP 46

24. GOURMET CHICKEN CAESAR WRAP 47

25. THAI LIME PORK WRAPS 48

26. AVOCADO SHRIMP WRAP 49

27. CHICKEN LEMON CABBAGE WRAPS 50

28. SPINACH CHEESE WRAP 51

29. SAUSAGE AND PEPPER WRAP 52

30. SWEET POTATO BURRITO CARAMELIZED ONIONS 53

31. PALEO STYLE COCONUT CHICKEN 54

32. ANCESTRAL ROASTED CHICKEN 55

33. PALEO PINEAPPLE CHICKEN SLOW COOKER RECIPE 57

34. PALEO LIME, CILANTRO AND CHILI CHICKEN SLOW COOKER RECIPE 58

35. PALEO CHICKEN TIKKA MASALA SLOW COOKER RECIPE 60

36. PORTUGUESE STYLE CHICKEN.. 62

37. SLOW-COOKED CHICKEN SPANISH STYLE 64

38. CHICKEN DRUMSTICKS TANDOORI & MANGO CHUTNEY 65

39. ORANGE CHICKEN PALEO STYLE 67

40. PALEO GREEK STYLE CHICKEN... 68

41. PALEO GREEK LEMON CHICKEN 70

42. VEGGIE STEW FROM JAMAICA 72

43. ROASTED BEEF WITH NUTTY VEGETABLES 74

44. PALEO SAUSAGE DELIGHT 76

45. PORK CHOPS WITH APPLE... 77

46. PALEO SPICY CHIPOTLE BEEF BRISKET SLOW COOKER RECIPE..................... 78

47. PALEO ASIAN INSPIRED PEPPER STEAK SLOW COOKER RECIPE.................... 80

48. PALEO SWEET AND SPICY SLOW COOKER CARNITAS 82

49. PALEO MEATBALLS AND SPAGHETTI SQUASH SLOW COOKER RECIPE 84

50. NUTTY TILAPIA FILLETS... 85

51. TILAPIA WITH THAI CURRY 86

52. STUFFED SEA BASS.. 88

53. CREAMY SALMON BAKE 89

54. LIME AND COCONUT SHRIMP THAI STYLE 90
55. PEAS AND HAM THICK SOUP 92
56. CHICKEN BACON CROCK POT CHOWDER 94
57. SPECIAL PALEO SOUP 96
58. TOMATO AND BASIL SOUP 97
59. PALEO CHICKEN SOUP 98
60. DELICIOUS CAULIFLOWER SOUP 99
61. PALEO BEEF SOUP 100
62. ROOT PALEO SOUP 101
63. DELIGHTFUL CHICKEN SOUP 102
64. PALEO LEMON AND GARLIC SOUP 103
65. RICH PALEO SOUP 104
66. PALEO VEGGIE SOUP 105
67. EMERALD CITY SOUP 106
68. PUMPKIN AND CHORIZO SOUP 107
69. ORANGE GINGER SQUASH SOUP 108
70. PURPLE SWEET POTATO SOUP 110
71. CREAMY COCONUT GREEN CHILI CHICKEN SOUP 111
72. THAI COCONUT TURKEY SOUP 113
73. CARROT SOUP 115
74. ASPARAGUS SALAD 116
75. PALEO ROASTED BROCCOLI SALAD 117
76. PALEO FENNEL APPLE SLAW 118
77. PALEO APPLE, PEAR, AND WALNUT SALAD 119
78. PALEO MEXICAN CHOPPED SALAD 120
79. PALEO BUTTERNUT SQUASH AND SPINACH SALAD 121
80. SALMON, SPINACH & APPLE SALAD 122
81. THE BIG SALAD 123
82. PARSLEY AND PEAR SMOOTHIE 124
83. PALEO PEACH AND COCONUT SMOOTHIE 125
84. GRAPES & WATERMELON SMOOTHIE 126
85. BLUEBERRY PEAR SMOOTHIE 127
86. BANANA-PEAR SMOOTHIE 128
87. ASPARAGUS-PEAR SMOOTHIE 129
88. BLUEBERRY ASPARAGUS-PEAR SMOOTHIE 130
89. GINGER GREEN SMOOTHIE 131
90. CALMING COCONUT SMOOTHIE 132
91. ANTI-INFLAMMATORY SMOOTHIE 133

92. Berry Anti-Inflammatory Smoothie 134
93. Beets'n'Nuts Smoothie 135
94. Cauliflangonut Smoothie 136
95. Red And White Smoothie 137
96. Cauliflower Power Smoothie 138

SPECIFIC CARBOHYDRATE DIET RECIPES 139

1. Almond Flour Waffles 140
2. Baked Eggs in Harissa Spice 141
3. Breakfast Muffins 142
4. Legal French Toast 143
5. Banana Muffins 145
6. Grain-Free SCD Waffles 146
7. Breakfast Cereal Grain-Free 147
8. Zucchini Frittata Breakfast Muffins 148
9. Cauliflower Bites & Chili 149
10. SCD Beef Borritos 150
11. Beef, Eggplant, Celery & Peppers Stew 152
12. Chicken & Onion Stew 153
13. Zucchini Rolls 154
14. Beef Pot Roast with Broccoli 155
15. Mixed Seafood, Saffron & Sundried Tomatoes 156
16. Sloppy Joe Baked Sweet Potatoes 157
17. Cauliflower Soup with Roasted Brussels Sprouts 158
18. Turkey Taco Lettuce Wraps 159
19. Canned Tuna Ceviche 160
20. California Grilled Chicken with Vinaigrette Dressing 161
21. Blueberry Chicken Salad 162
22. Steak Kebabs with Chimichurri 163
23. Garlic Shrimp with Tomatoes 164
24. Thai Coconut Shrimp Curry 165
25. Spiced Flounder with Tomatoes 166
26. Beef, Cabbage, and Tomato Soup 167
27. Cuban Picadillo 168
28. Chicken and Sweet Potato 169
29. Teriyaki Chicken & Carrots 170
30. Spicy Beef Stew –Korean Style 171

31. CACCIUCCO - SHRIMP, MUSSELS, FISH & SCALLOPS STEW 172
32. CHICKEN STOCK 173
33. SWEET POTATO SOUP 174
34. TACO SOUP 175
35. MUSHROOM BURGERS 177
36. BEEF RAGU 178
37. CORNED BEEF IN THE SLOW-COOKER 179
38. GROUND BEEF STIR FRY 180
39. MARINARA BEEF ROAST 181
40. MEATBALLS IN A HURRY 182
41. TACO CASSEROLE 183
42. VENISON BURGERS 184
43. CHICKEN TENDERS 185
44. CHILI ROASTED CHICKEN THIGHS 186
45. INDIAN STYLE CHICKEN DRUMSTICKS 187
46. SWEET POTATO AND SAUSAGE CASSEROLE 188
47. CHICKEN AND AVOCADO SALAD 189
48. PINEAPPLE AND PORK STIR-FRY 190
49. FRUIT CAKE 191
50. RASPBERRY, WATERMELON AND MINT SALAD 193
51. EGG IN A JAR 194
52. THAI PORK LETTUCE WRAPS 195
53. STUFFED CALAMARI 196
54. FRUIT PUDDING 198
55. LEMON CHICKEN STIR FRY 199
56. PAN SEARED BRUSSELS SPROUTS 200
57. MACADAMIA HUMMUS WITH VEGETABLES 201
58. BEEF GOULASH 202
59. BAKED BEEF WITH VEGETABLES 204
60. QUICK CHOCOLATE BONBON 205
61. CHERRY AND ALMOND BUTTER MILKSHAKE 206
62. GINGER BROWNIES 207
63. WATERMELON & KIWI WITH FRESH HERBS 208
64. SCD BEEF BORRITOS 209
65. ROASTED TOMATOES 210
66. SPECIFIC CARBOHYDRATE DIET GUACAMOLE 211
67. PULLED HAWAIIAN PORK 212
68. SCD SHRIMP SCAMPI 213

69. Eggs Baked in Avocado 214

70. Awesome Blossom Cauliflower 215

71. Bacon Wrapped Steak with Onions and Mushrooms 216

72. Roasted Brussels Sprouts in Avocado Oil with Orange and Pomegranate 217

73. Thai Style Carrot Soup 218

74. Peanut Butter Cookies 219

75. SCD Legal Sandwich Bread 220

CONCLUSION 222

Description

Before you have even purchased or downloaded this book I'm pretty confident, you've read or heard of the Paleo Diet and the SCD diet at least once or twice. Well, that's because the Paleo Diet has gained popularity for being one of the healthiest fitness diets with celebrities, athletes, and other cross-fitters following the principles of Paleo. The SCD diet has also gained huge popularity online amongst people suffering from Crohn's Disease and Colitis and other Ailments as the healthier choice for eating when the normal American diet is not working for them.

Proponents of this life changing diet believe that the dawn of the Agricultural Age has changed the way man ate. From being meat eaters, men became more dependent on farm-raised foods (grains, pasta, bread, and other carb-rich foods) which were very different from what the cavemen ate. The problem here is that, although man's diet changed, our genetic makeup has not evolved over the last thousands of years, and this means that our bodies are still not accustomed to most of the foods available today.

Processed foods and large food servings are also seen as the primary culprits as to why the statistics of overweight individuals have been ballooning over the decades.

The Paleo Diet works by simply re-programming our diet to what it was originally designed. By eliminating "unnatural foods" such as carb-rich, processed, high fat and sugar laden foods, Paleo can help you to be more fit and strong like our cavemen ancestors.

The SCD (Specific Carbohydrate Diet) works by simply eliminating non-digestible carbohydrates that not only feed the bad bacteria in your colon but promote and induce leaky gut syndrome therefore creating an autoimmune condition in your system.

The SCD has been popularized for the huge success it has had with people suffering from these debilitating illness and helping them with fewer symptoms, and some even getting into a state of remission with their disease.

Introduction to the Paleo Diet

Also known as the "Caveman Diet," the Paleo Diet is a nutrient-rich food regimen patterned from the diet of our hunter-gatherer ancestors (cavemen) of the Paleolithic Era. The principle of Paleo is simple: avoid the type of foods which were not available during the Paleolithic Era which means that "modern food" (grains, farm-grown meat, dairy, sweets, processed food, etc.) had been eliminated in the Paleo Diet.

Farming made us believe that to be satiated, the majority of our diet must be made of carbohydrate rich foods. This high-carb diet, however, is seen to be a major contributor as to why man's physique has regressed from being fit to fat. When carbohydrates are consumed, our body transforms them into glucose, which is used as energy. However, when glucose is not burned as energy, it turns into body fat, and this explains why people who live sedentary lifestyles have extra pounds of fat! Physical activities are essential to burn the carbs which you consume.

Although Paleo has only become popular in the 2000's, it was actually in the early 1900s, 1913 to be exact, when Joseph Knowles suggested a healthier diet after a two-month experiment living in the wilderness. Knowles claimed that he became more fit and stronger after living as a hunter-gatherer, like that of our cavemen ancestors.

This idea was followed a few decades after when gastroenterologist, Dr. Walter L. Voegtin coined the term "Paleo Diet" in his book The Stone Age Diet which was published in 1975. In his book, Voegtin's suggests that 99.9% of the modern man's genetic code came from our hunter-gatherer ancestors, and this means that our bodies naturally survive on a diet like that of our ancestors from the Stone Age.

This idea has also gained the interest of a few scientists and anthropologists who also published research papers about the diet. However, it was only in the year 2013 when the Paleo Diet gained immense popularity from the public after nutrition expert Loren Cordain launched the Paleo Diet Movement.

Introduction to the Specific Carbohydrate Diet

Specific Carbohydrate Diet is a diet designed specifically for Crohn's disease, Ulcerative Colitis, IBD and IBS. While a popular cure for these targeted areas, it has many amazing benefits for anyone wishing to have a healthy and well-balanced life. With a track record of curing thousands of individuals suffering from some form of bowel disease, the foods are eaten within this diet are known to boost your quality of life.

The SCD is a gluten-free, grain-free, lactose-free, and refined sugar-free diet. Although this diet may seem similar to the no carb diet, it does not fully eliminate sweets and dairy. The carbs that are considered "short-chain carbohydrates" are what is allowed on this diet. Short chain carbohydrates are fruit, honey, homemade yogurt, nuts, and legal vegetables.

What's wrong with the Modern Diet

As you now know, the basic idea of the Paleo Diet is to avoid all types of food which were not available during the Stone Age. So what's wrong with the "modern diet"?

Simply by comparing the physical state of an average caveman to an average modern-day man, you can already see that cavemen were lean, strong, and agile while the modern man is physically unfit and sluggish. What could be the reason why man has transitioned from being fit to becoming overweight?

The modern diet consists of nothing but packaged and processed foods. All you have to do is look at your typical grocery chain. When you walk in you will see 10-14 isles of nothing but food packaged in boxes and containers of some sort, and maybe an isle or two of fresh foods such as vegetables, fruits and fresh meats. Typical American has a very poor diet that consists of mainly processed foods laced with tons of sugars, fats, sodiums and large amounts of hidden harmful ingredients.

The typical diet consists of a cup or two of coffee in the morning with a donut, then for lunch a burger with fries and then for dinner they will throw in a microwavable dinner in. You see it's all garbage all processed food nothing fresh nothing live, just empty calories that don't fuel the body with the right nutrients and minerals that the body requires for good vibrant health.

Why you Should Start on these Diets

Starting any diet plan or changing your food routine in order to alter your lifestyle can be challenging. In order to gain the most from your experience on the SCD or Paleo Diet, it's important to plan accordingly and know all the ins and outs of the diet. Staying motivated, encouraged, and educated throughout the process is not only recommended, but required to succeed.

If you're an avid junk food eater, or just the average American, switching to this diet will take some getting used to. The SCD or Paleo Diet consists of the healthiest, most organic and wholesome foods. Thus, you'll not only help you mintain a healthy gut, but will have the ability to stay strong and energetic, with lasting health benefits.

Additionally, if you are looking to embark on this journey, it's important to ask yourself why you want to do this. Having a concrete plan and a main goal or objective will keep you on the right track. Especially for people will low will-power or a history of excessive weight gain, maintaining the correct mindset will prove beneficial in the long run.

It's normal for people to struggle with weight loss techniques and various diet plans when appetizing temptations are everywhere we look. Particularly on this diet, where fried, cheesy, and delicious bread are to be avoided. Thus, there are several tips you can follow in order to stay on track and focused.

#1 Have a friend join you

Support systems are always encouraged on diet plans. Sticking to a limited number of foods can be tricky when attending events, parties, and other gatherings. Having a friend who is going through the same process will alleviate some of the stress for you and in turn make the task a fun and inclusive affair. Plus, you'll be able to exchange recipes and maybe he/she is a phenomenal cook willing to share!

#2 Prepare yourself properly

You know your schedule and how likely you are to be tempted, especially when you're hungry. It's essential to buy food in advance and even prepare it early if you know you won't have any time later. Being left with an empty stomach or no time will lead to bad food choices and you'll stray from the diet. If you are headed to an event where you know there will be a lack of fresh Paleo food, try bringing your own snack or even a dish to share! Just because it's healthy doesn't mean people won't like it. Most people just opt for other unhealthy alternatives because they are fast, easy, and all-American favorites. A yummy guacamole dip or a meat and veggie dish will sure be a crowd pleaser. You may even recruit prospective Paleo goers!

#3 Set a goal

When times get tough, you may want to resort to a cheat meal or indulge in something non-Paleo. To avoid this, it's important to set a goal early on in the diet plan and stick with it. You need to assess whether this is a short-term process, or if you will be continuing the diet for an extended amount of time. It may also be useful to physically write down your goals for the diet and specific reasons to go SCD or Paleo. Put this list somewhere accessible and where you will be able to see it on a daily basis. Remind yourself that when working towards a goal, every single day counts!

#4 Stay faithful to your diet!

No matter who you are, temptation on diets is always prevalent. However, if you never take a quick bite of a snack in the first place, it will be easier to avoid it altogether. When you start cheating on your diet, you may be inclined to keep indulging in that snack. If you simply can't resist however, take a small serving of it and walk away. For instance, a small piece of dark chocolate or a healthy non-Paleo or SCD food will do. If you find yourself completely off track for one day, start fresh the next morning. Don't deprive yourself and start your day with a killer Paleo breakfast.

#5 Record you're eating habits

If you are notorious for overeating, even on diets, it may be best to record the foods that you are consuming. Even though the Paleo diet contains all healthy foods, you should still be eating them in moderation. Frequently snacking in-between meals can really rack up the calories and can delay the weight loss process. If this is something you seem to struggle with or not, writing down everything you consume in a food diary will prove interesting and provide insight. This will increase your likelihood of succeeding and will help you reach your goal.

#6 Get enough sleep and move around

Getting an ample amount of sleep each night will ultimately help your mood and will encourage weight loss. Sleep deprivation can often cause irritation and fatigue, which has you opting for unhealthy alternatives. Additionally, constantly moving around and seeing progress from exercise will motivate you to make continue your diet and put healthy foods into your body.

#7 Track your progress

Although not encouraged for everyone on this diet, frequent weigh-ins can be useful for some of you! Writing down daily progress reports or creating a chart can create a sort of game for you and ultimately prompt enthusiastic participation in this diet. Some people create small and large goals, and reward themselves when progress occurs.

Benefits of the SCD & Paleo Diet

Eating wholesome foods, vegetables and fruits are promoted in the SCD and Paleo diet providing your body with the required minerals, salts and vitamins. This has a positive effect on your health. Let us find out about the various benefits of the Paleo diet.

1. Improves dental health

Acid producing bacteria that cause damage to the teeth are reduced when this diet is followed. Vitamins A, D and K help in the repair of tissue while calcium helps in strengthening the bones and minimizing decay. Anti-inflammatory properties that can relieve symptoms of periodontal diseases are found in vitamin C.

2. Reduces allergies

As allergens in your food are reduced the allergies also go down. Eliminating dairy products and grains helps control allergies as eating anti-inflammatory foods helps to control the inflammation that leads to allergic responses.

3. Decreases inflammation

The high presence of anti-inflammatory properties in the Paleo diet decreases the risk of cardiovascular diseases which can be caused due to inflammation. Both gut and cardiovascular inflammation

4. Helps tackle diabetes

Lack of refined sugar, minimum fat intake promoted in this diet helps in keeping the sugar levels in check.

5. Helps in better sleep

As you cut down on chemicals and additives by following the Paleo diet, you will find that you feel naturally tired by night and feel the need to sleep. Serotonin, released by the brain, is not overridden by chemicals and your body picks up the sleep signals better.

6. Helps in weight loss

The Paleo diet is naturally nutrient dense and low in carbohydrates. Eliminating processed food will help you to lose weight.

7. Decreases risk of cancer

Scientific evidence shows that foods containing phytonutrients and antioxidants as found in the Paleo diet help fight diseases like cancer.

8.   Strengthens hair

The nutrient density of the food consumed in the Paleo diet leads to improved thickness, strength and shine of your hair. Zinc and iron, present in red meat and shellfish and biotin present in eggs are great for maintaining healthy hair and nails.

9.   Keeps acne problems in control

A Paleo diet directly addresses the most common reasons for skin problems which are, inflammation, nutrient deficiencies and gut dysbiosis. Excessive omega-6 fat present in refined oils causes inflammation. This is eliminated in the Paleo diet leading to a reduction of problems like acne, eczema and psoriasis.

10.   Increases energy levels

Refined foods are absorbed quickly producing adrenal fatigue. With the Paleo diet, you eat foods with low glycemic index. The sugars in such foods are absorbed slowly, hence a lag in energy is avoided and you feel energetic throughout the day.

Do's and Don'ts

To make it easier for you to choose what to eat, refer to the list below:

What to Eat...

Fruits

Vegetables

Seafood

Grass-fed Meat

Healthy Fats

Nuts and Seeds

What Not To Eat...

Grains

Dairy

Sugars (unnatural)

Processed Foods

Starches

Legumes

Alcohol

As a rule of thumb, stick to foods that are whole, raw, and unprocessed. Stay away from GMO food and processed food products. Always read the labels. If it contains more than three ingredients and you can't even read them, do not take it.

Grocery list

Condiments

- Capers in brine or oil
- Mustard

  Brown or Russian mustard
- Dijon or yellow mustard
- Grainy or English mustard
- Fish sauce
- Kalamata olives in brine or oil
- Mayonnaise, preferably homemade (to ensure that individual ingredients are all Paleo or SCD safe)
- Pesto, preferably homemade (to ensure that it remains dairy-free)
- Salt
- Kosher salt
- Pink Himalayan salt
- Sea salt
- Vinaigrettes, preferably homemade (to ensure that these do not contain sweeteners)
- Vinegar – almost all vinegar products are Paleo safe, but there are a few manufacturers who try to pass off really cheap ones by adding food coloring and sugar. Read product labels before buying.
- Apple cider vinegar
- Balsamic vinegar
- Black currant vinegar
- Cane vinegar
- Coconut vinegar
- Date vinegar
- Jujube vinegar

- Kiwi fruit vinegar
- Malt vinegar
- Palm vinegar
- Persimmon vinegar
- Pomegranate vinegar
- Quince vinegar
- Raisin vinegar
- Raspberry vinegar
- Rice vinegar / rice wine vinegar / mirin
- Tomato vinegar
- Wolfberry vinegar

Fats and Oils

- Avocado oil (not suitable for cooking, but great for making vinaigrettes, and drizzling over meat and vegetables)
- Bacon drippings or bacon grease (from Paleo-safe bacon, store-bought or homemade)
- Clarified butter or ghee
- Coconut butter and coconut oil
- Duck fat (use as sparingly as possible)
- Flaxseed oil (same properties as avocado oil)
- Macadamia oil (same properties as avocado oil)
- Olive oil / extra virgin olive oil

Flours

Although there are Paleo-safe flours and starches, it would be best to use or consume these sparingly, especially if you are trying to lose weight, or if you are trying to control your blood sugar and insulin levels. Aside from almond flour/meal and coconut flour, (both are medium flours), you can also safely use:

- Light flours. These work well as binders and thickening agents, and may be safely used as cornstarch substitute. However, these cannot be used to make baked goods (e.g. bread, pies, etc.) on their own. Light flours cannot hold their shape during prolonged cooking or baking, and must be mixed with medium or dense flours. These include:
- Arrowroot powder
- Ground chia seeds
- Ground flaxseeds and/or flaxseed meal
- Kuzu starch
- Sweet potato starch (usually white colored; not to be confused with sweet potato powder)

- Medium flours. These can be used as binders and thickening agents as well, but these can also be used in baking. These flours provide elasticity (bounce) to bread, and can be successfully kneaded and proofed. These include:
- Chestnut flour
- Ground plantain and plantain flour (have distinct plantain flavor)
- Ground pumpkin
- Ground sweet potato
- Ground taro
- Ground winter squash
- Ground yucca
- Pumpkin seed flour
- Sweet potato powder (distinctly orange colored, not to be confused with sweet potato starch)
- Tapioca flour/starch
- Dense flours. These should always be combined with light or medium flours when baking as these need inordinate amounts of baking powder and/or baking soda to rise properly. These include:
- Cashew flour
- Hazelnut flour (has mild hazelnut flavor)
- Macadamia nut flour

- Pecan flour

- Sunflower seed flour

- Walnut flour

Now Let us share some of the recipes you can use while following the Paleo diet or SCD and help you reach your goal of a healthier gut and healthy body.

Paleo recipes

(Caution , if your very sensitive to the use of peppers please use with caution, in most digestive disorders require very moderate use of peppers , it is advisable to reduce amount of peppers and some other ingredients for those suffering from Crohn's or Colitis)*

1.Heavenly Ham n' Eggs

Prep Time: 5 minutes

Cooking time: 15 minutes

Ingredients:

4 slices of ham

2 eggs

(Spices for flavor)

Procedures:

1. Preheat your oven to 400°F
2. Prepare a muffin pan by greasing it with coconut oil.
3. Place two pieces of ham on top of each other in one muffin cup. Repeat with the next muffin cup.
4. Crack the egg on top of the ham
   (Optional: add scallions, basil, etc.   On top your eggs for more flavor.
5. Bake for 15 minutes and serve.

2. Supper Veggie Omelette

Prep Time: 15 minutes
Cooking Time: 20 minutes

Ingredients

4 eggs
30 ml (2 tablespoons) olive oil
1 onion, chopped
1 garlic clove, minced
125 ml (½ cup) carrots, thinly sliced
125 ml (½ cup) red bell pepper, deseeded, julienne
1 zucchini, thinly sliced
125 ml (½ cup) baby spinach, chopped
15 ml (1 tablespoon) fresh basil, chopped
Sea salt and freshly ground pepper to taste
Fresh parsley, chopped for sprinkle

Procedures:

1. In a bowl, whisk the eggs vigorously until fluffy, about 2 minutes.
2. Heat oil in a frying non-stick pan, sauté onions and garlic for 2-3 minutes on high heat until tender.
3. Lower the heat to medium. Add red bell peppers, zucchini, spinach and tomatoes. Cook for 5 minutes until vegetables are crisply tender. Add eggs and basil. Season with salt and pepper to taste. Cook for 10-15 minutes on medium low heat until the eggs are done.
4. Cut into wedges, sprinkle with parsley, and serve hot.

3. Veggie-bun Sandwich

Prep Time: 5 minutes
Cooking Time: 0 minutes

Ingredients:

1 pc. Red bell pepper
2 slices turkey ham
½ avocado (cut into strips)
1 pc. Seaweed strips

Procedures:

1. Take the bell pepper and slice it in half and remove the seeds.
2. Take one piece of bell pepper and top it with the ham, seaweed, and avocado.
3. Top with the other half of the bell pepper and stick a toothpick in the center. Enjoy.

4. Turkey Low carb Paleo Patties

Prep Time: 5 minutes

Cooking Time: 0 minutes

Ingredients:

16 oz. ground lean turkey

1 tsp. paprika

½ tsp. coriander

1 tsp. powdered onion

Pinch of cayenne pepper

Pinch of salt

Pinch of ground pepper

2 pcs. Green onions (chopped)

1 pc. Tomato (sliced)

2 cups arugula

1 pc. Avocado (sliced)

Procedures:

1. In a bowl, place the ground turkey and add the onion powder, salt, pepper, paprika, cayenne pepper, and green onions and combine everything.
2. Use your hands to form into burger patties.
3. Heat the grill and cook the burgers for 5 minutes, per side.
4. Place the cooked patties over the arugula, tomatoes, and avocado. Serve.
5. Kale Breakfast Muffin and 8oz of water

5. Kale Breakfast Muffin

Prep Time: 5 minutes
Cooking Time: 0 minutes

Ingredients:

½ cup kale (finely chopped)

1/8 cup onion chives (finely chopped)

¼ cup almond milk

3 eggs

4 slices of smoked turkey

Pepper to taste

Procedures:

1. Preheat oven to 350°F
2. In a mixing bowl, whisk together the eggs, kale, chives, almond milk and sprinkle with pepper to taste.
3. Take a muffin pan and grease it with coconut oil. Fill the muffin cups with two slices of smoked turkey each and fill 2/3 of it with the kale mixture.
4. Bake for 30 minutes. Let it cool and serve.

6. Almond Flour Blueberry Waffles

Prep Time: 15 minutes

Cooking Time: 12-15 minutes

Ingredients:

250 ml (1 cup) blueberries

3 eggs, separated

250 ml (1 cup) almond flour

60 ml (¼ cup) almond milk

1 teaspoon vanilla extract

30 ml (2 tablespoons) olive oil

Raw honey to sprinkle on top

Procedures:

1. Grease the waffle maker with olive oil or coconut butter, and pre-heat it.
In a mixing bowl, using a hand electric beater, whisk the egg whites on high speed until the form stiff peaks, about 2-3 minutes.
In another bowl, combine the egg yolks, the almond milk, and vanilla extract. Add the coconut flour and salt and olive oil. Mix well until you have a smooth batter.
Incorporate 1/3 of the egg whites into the batter, mixing well. Add another 1/3 of the egg whites, and fold it into the batter until they are well incorporated. Repeat. You should have a light and fluffy batter.
Pour about 1/2 cup of the batter into the waffle maker, close the lid, and let it cook according to the manufacturer instructions. .
To serve, top each waffle with blueberries, and drizzle with maple syrup or raw honey.

7. Raspberry-Almond Pancakes

Prep Time: 10 minutes
Cooking Time: 10 minutes

Ingredients:

250 ml (1 cup) fresh raspberries
4 eggs
250 ml (1 cup) almond meal
125 ml (½ cup) unsweetened almond milk
1 teaspoon vanilla extract
10 ml (2 teaspoons) baking powder
2.5 ml (½ teaspoon) ground cinnamon
30 ml (2 tablespoons) coconut oil
30 ml (2 tablespoons) olive oil
Maple syrup for drizzle or fresh fruits with raw honey for garnish

Procedures:

1. In a bowl, whisk together the raspberries and the eggs.
2. Mix in almond milk, olive oil and vanilla extract
3. In another bowl, whisk together almond meal, baking powder, and cinnamon.
4. Gradually add the dry ingredients with the egg and blueberries. Combine well using a whisk.
5. Melt the coconut butter in a medium-sized frying pan on high heat. Spoon about 30 ml (2 tablespoons) of the batter into the pan. Cook for 2-3 minutes or until slightly golden on each side.
6. Drizzle with maple syrup or fresh fruits with raw honey for garnish and serve.

8. Cucumber Sandwich

Prep Time: 5 minutes

Cooking Time: 0 minutes

Ingredients:

1 pc. Cucumber
3 turkey breast slices (low sodium)
Dijon mustard
Garlic and herb spreadable

Procedures:

1. Take the cucumber and cut in half. Remove the seeds.
2. Spread the garlic and herb on cucumber.
3. Add the turkey slices on top and drizzle with Dijon mustard.
4. Sandwich with the other half of the cucumber. Enjoy.

9. Berry-coconut Shake

Prep Time: 5 minutes

Cooking Time: 0 minutes

Ingredients:

8 pcs. Frozen strawberries
1 cup coconut milk
1 tsp. honey
1 tsp. almond butter
2 pcs. Fresh strawberries
Coconut shavings

Procedures:

1. Blend the strawberries, coconut milk, honey and almond butter.
2. Top with sliced fresh strawberries and coconut shavings

10. Southern-France Style Scrambled Eggs

Prep Time: 5 minutes

Cooking Time: 10 minutes

Ingredients:

125 ml (½ cup) onions, chopped
125 ml (½ cup) tomatoes, chopped
4 eggs
125 ml (½ cup) fresh basil leaves, chopped
2.5 ml (½ teaspoon) dried Provençale herb mix
Sea salt and freshly ground pepper to taste
30 ml (2 tablespoons) coconut oil

Procedures:

1. In a mixing bowl, whisk the eggs until fluffy. Add Provençale herbs.
2. Melt the coconut oil in a medium frying pan, Add onions, and sauté for 2-3 minutes until the onions are fragrant and tender. Add tomatoes and basil leaves. Season with salt and pepper.
3. Add eggs to the pan, and cook for 3-5 minutes until the eggs are not runny anymore, stirring occasionally to scramble the eggs.
4. Serve hot with paleo-approved breakfast sausages or bacon strips, if desired.

11. Fancy-Applesauce Paleo Pancakes

Prep Time: 10 minutes

Cooking Time: 10 minutes

Ingredients

250 ml (1 cup) unsweetened applesauce, preferably homemade or organic

250 ml (1 cup) almond meal

3 eggs

60 ml (¼ cup) almond milk

2.5 ml (½ teaspoon) baking powder

5 ml (1 teaspoon) vanilla extract

1 ml (¼ teaspoon) ground nutmeg

1 ml (¼ teaspoon) ground cinnamon

30 ml (2 tablespoons) melted coconut oil

Olive oil for frying

Procedures:

1. Beat eggs and applesauce together in a mixing bowl. Add vanilla, almond milk, olive oil.
2. Mix almond milk and vanilla extract with egg and potatoes.
3. In another bowl, mix together almond meal, baking powder, ground nutmeg and ground cinnamon.
4. Gradually add the dry ingredients to the eggs mixture, and combine well.
5. Heat about 1 tablespoon of olive oil in a medium frying non-stick pan. When the oil is hot, spoon about 60 ml (1/4 cup) of this batter into the pan, and cook for 2-3 minutes on each side until slightly golden.
6. Serve the pancakes hot with a drizzle of organic maple syrup or fresh fruits with raw honey.

12. Hash-Caveman Style Breakfast

Prep Time: 15 minutes

Cooking Time: 25 minutes

Ingredients:

For the sausage patties

450 g (1 pound) of ground pork or veal

1-2 garlic cloves, minced

2.5 ml (½ teaspoon) jalapeños, minced or 1 ml (¼ teaspoon) crushed hot chilies flakes

2.5 ml (½ teaspoon) dry thyme

2.5 ml (½ teaspoon) dry rosemary

1 ml (¼ teaspoon) fennel seeds

1 egg

Sea salt and freshly ground pepper to taste

For the hash (all ingredients to be chopped should be about the same size)

4 paleo-approved bacon strip, diced

4 breakfast sausages, homemade or paleo approved, diced

4 eggs

1 tablespoons olive oil (optional)

1 yellow onion, diced

1 green bell pepper, diced

1 red bell pepper, diced

2 celery stalks, diced

1 sweet potato, diced

1 zucchini, diced

2 garlic cloves, minced

1 tablespoon jalapeños pepper, minced

Sea salt and fresh ground pepper to taste

Procedures:

Pre-heat the oven to 200°C/400 F.

For the sausage patties:

1. Place all the ingredients in a mixing bowl and combine well. Let rest and cover with a plastic wrap for at least 30 minutes. Form equal sized patties.
2. In a large frying pan, heat some olive oil on high heat. Fry the patties until well done, about 3-4 minutes on each side on medium-high heat. Do not press down too much on the patties while cooking or they will harden.

3. *For the hash*

4. In a large skillet, cook the bacon over high heat for 2-3 minutes until golden. Add onions and garlic, and continue cooking on medium heat for 2-3 minutes. Add sweet potatoes, cook for 5-6 minutes until the bacon is cooked. Add remaining ingredients. Cook for additional 5-6 minutes or until all the vegetables are tender crisp. Season with salt and pepper to taste. Remove the pan from heat and reserve.
5. In another frying pan, cook the eggs sunny side up until done. Season with salt and pepper to taste
6. Spoon ¼ of the hash on a plate, top with one sunny egg. Repeat for each serving.

13. *Paleo Style Granola Bars*

Prep Time: 5 minutes

Cooking Time: 15 minutes

Refrigerating time: 1 hour

Ingredients:

30 ml (2 tablespoons) pumpkin seeds

30 ml (2 tablespoons) poppy seeds

30 ml (2 tablespoons) sunflower seeds

30 ml (2 tablespoons) sesame seeds

30 ml (2 tablespoons) almonds, sliced

60 ml (4 tablespoons) freshly squeezed orange juice

15 ml (1 tablespoon) coconut oil

30 ml (2 tablespoons) raw honey

Procedures:

1. Preheat oven to 180°C/350°F. Lightly grease a baking dish with olive oil.
2. Combine all ingredients in a bowl and seasons with salt and pepper.
3. Spread batter over a baking dish.
4. Bake for 10 to 15 minutes or until golden browned. Remove from oven and let it cool.
5. Cut into bars and refrigerate for at least 1 hour until set before serving.

14. *Apple-Spicey Muffins*

Prep time: 15 minutes

Cooking time: 20 minutes

Ingredients:

2 cups almond flour

2 teaspoons baking powder

3 apples, peeled and shredded

2 tablespoons maple syrup

¾ cup coconut milk

2 large eggs

2 tablespoons coconut oil

1 teaspoon cinnamon

1/8 teaspoon nutmeg

Vegetable cooking spray

Procedures:

1. Preheat your oven to 180°C/350°F. Grease muffin tin with cooking spray.
2. In a bowl, mix dry ingredients together well.
3. In another bowl, mix all wet ingredients, until well combined. Add the mixture to the dry ingredients and whisk well.
4. Add the minced apple to the batter and mix well. Pour the batter into each the muffin hole until they are 3/4 full.
5. Bake for around 18-20 minutes, until cooked thoroughly. You can check by inserting a toothpick in the middle of one of the muffin.

15. Paleo Pumpkin Muffins

Prep Time: 2 minutes

Cooking Time: 25 minutes

Ingredients:

750 ml (1½ cup) almond flour

60 ml (4 tablespoons) coconut flour

5 ml (1 teaspoon) baking soda

5 ml (1 teaspoon) baking powder

2.5 ml (½ teaspoon) pumpkin pie spice

2.5 ml (½ teaspoon) ground cinnamon

0.5 ml (⅛ teaspoon) sea salt

2 large eggs

¾ cup pumpkin puree

60 ml (¼ cup) raw honey

30 ml (2 teaspoons) almond butter

15 ml (1 tablespoon) almonds, toasted and chopped

Procedures:

1. Preheat the oven to 200°C/400°F.
2. Whisk almond flour, coconut flour, baking soda, baking powder, and pumpkin pie spice in a mixing bowl. Sprinkle with cinnamon and salt.
3. In another bowl whisk the eggs. Add pumpkin puree, honey, and butter.
4. Mix wet ingredients with dry ingredients. Fill the batter in muffin cups until each is almost full.
5. Sprinkle with almonds.

6. Bake for 20 to 25 minutes, or until a toothpick inserted in the center comes out clean.

16. Paleo Safe Beef Jerky

Prep Time: 10 minutes

Marinating Time: 2 hours or overnight

Cooking Time: 4 hours

Ingredients:

225 g (½ pound) flank steak

30 ml (2 tablespoons) Coconut Amino

1 garlic clove, mined

2.5 ml (½ teaspoon) smoked paprika

2.5 ml (½ teaspoon) chipotle powder

2.5 ml (½ teaspoon) onion powder

2.5 ml (½ teaspoon) ginger powder

2.5 ml (½ teaspoon) salt

2.5 ml (½ teaspoon) black pepper

Procedures:

1. Preheat the oven to 60ºC/170°F. Lightly grease a baking dish.
2. Combine all ingredients in a bowl and mix together.
3. Leave marinated for at least 2 hours or overnight.
4. Put stake in the baking dish and bake for 3 to 4 hours.

17. Paleo Honey Butter Roasted Walnuts Slow Cooker Recipe

Prep Time: 10 mins.

Cook Time: 2 hours

Ingredients:

¼ cup of honey

½ teaspoon of pumpkin pie spice

3 tablespoons of grass fed butter

2 cups of raw walnuts

1 teaspoon of vanilla extract

Procedures:

1. Place the grass fed butter directly in the slow cooker.

2. Turn the slow cooker on high and allow the heat to melt the butter.

3. After the butter melts, add the pumpkin pie spice, honey and vanilla to the butter, mixing together until ingredients are well combined.

4. Add the walnuts to the slow cooker and use a wooden spoon to toss the nuts until they are well coated with the butter and honey mixture.

5. Allow nuts to cook on high for 1-2 hours. You should check the walnuts from time to time, opening the lid and stirring them every half hour to ensure you do not burn the walnuts on the bottom of the slow cooker. Do not allow nuts to overcook.

6. Remove from slow cooker and enjoy. Leftovers can be stored in the refrigerator as long as they are placed in an airtight container.

18. *Mixed Spicy Nuts*

Prep Time: 5 minutes

Cooking Time: 0 minutes

Ingredients:

5 ml (1 teaspoon) coconut oil

60 ml (¼ cup) pecans, toasted

60 ml (¼ cup) almonds, toasted

60 ml (¼ cup) walnuts, toasted

2.5 ml (½ teaspoon) chili powder

1 ml (¼ teaspoon) cumin

Pinch of salt and pepper

Procedures:

1. Toss all ingredients in a mixing bowl and season with salt and pepper.

19. Banana with Coconut & Almond Butter

Prep Time: 10 minutes

Cooking Time: 0 minutes

Ingredients:

2 bananas, sliced

60 ml (4 tablespoons) coconut milk

60 ml (4 tablespoons) almond butter

0.5 ml (⅛ teaspoon) cinnamon

Procedures:

1. Toss all ingredients in a mixing bowl, and sprinkle with cinnamon. Let it rest 5 minutes before serving in dessert bowls.

20. Coconut Whipped Cream

Prep Time: 5 minutes

Refrigerating Time: 2-3 hours

Ingredients:

250 ml (1 cup) coconut cream

250 ml (1 cup) coconut milk

1 ml (¼ teaspoon) cinnamon

2.5 ml (½ teaspoon) vanilla extract

1 ml (¼ teaspoon) ground nutmeg

Procedures:

1. Place all the ingredients in food processor, and blend until smooth and creamy.
2. Pour coconut cream into 4 cups, and refrigerate for at least 2 to 3 hours.
3. Serve and enjoy!

21. Paleo Pizza

Prep Time: 10 minutes

Cooking Time: 55 minutes

Ingredients

For crust:
1000 ml (4 cups) almond flour

2 eggs

45 ml (3 tablespoons) olive oil

5 ml (1 teaspoon) garlic powder

1 ml (¼ teaspoon) baking soda

2.5 ml (1½ tablespoon) fresh rosemary, chopped

For toppings:
250 ml (1 cup) organic marinara sauce

485 g (1 pound) Italian paleo pork sausage, sliced

250 ml (1 cup) yellow summer squash, diced

3 scallions, chopped

15 ml (1 tablespoon) basil leaves

2 small tomatoes, diced

125 ml (½ cup) roasted red peppers, diced

15 ml (1 tablespoon) black olives, sliced

Salt to taste

Procedures:
2. Preheat the oven to 180ºC/350º F. Lightly grease a pizza pan.
3. Place all the crust ingredients in a food processor and pulse until a dough forms.
4. Form a ball with the dough using your hands. Place the ball in the center of greased pizza pan. Then press the dough using your hands, patting and shaping it into a circle. Bake for 20 minutes or until cooked. Remove from oven. Let it cool.
5. In a bowl, add sausages, squash, scallions, basil, tomatoes, red pepper, olives and salt and mix till well combined.
6. Spread pizza base with marinara sauce. Top with sausage mixture.
7. Return to oven and bake again for 25 to 35 minutes or until top is lightly golden.

22. *Cashew Butter Banana Wrap*

Prep Time: 10 mins.

Ingredients:

1 cup cashews, soaked overnight

3 tbsp. sesame oil

¼ tsp. salt

2 bananas, peeled and sliced

4 flax wraps (gluten Free)

Procedures:

1. Place cashews, sesame oil, salt in food processor and mix, scrape sides of bowl intermittently to ensure a smooth mixture.
2. Spread each wrap with cashew butter, add banana and wrap it up for breakfast.

23. Smoked Salmon Eggs Wrap

Prep Time: 10 mins.

Ingredients:

4 slices smoked salmon

6 eggs

¼ cup radish, shredded

1 lemon, juiced

½ tsp. salt, pepper

4 almond wraps (gluten free)

Procedures:

1. Mix radish with lemon juice, set aside.
2. Whisk eggs with salt, pepper.
3. Heat 2 tbsp. extra virgin olive oil in nonstick pan.
4. Pour eggs into the pan and cook a minute per side.
5. Divide omelet into four sections. Place a quarter of omelet on the almond wrap, top with smoked salmon and shredded radish and roll.

24. Gourmet Chicken Caesar Wrap

Prep Time: 15 mins.

Ingredients:

1 lb. chicken breasts

3 tbsp. sardines, chopped

1 egg

1 tsp. dry mustard

½ lemon, juiced

2 cups green leaf lettuce, chopped

½ tsp. salt, black pepper

Extra virgin olive oil

Procedures:

1. Preheat oven to 375 degrees and lightly coat glass baking dish with olive oil.
2. Combine sardines, egg, dry mustard, lemon juice, salt and pepper in food processor and mix until creamy.
3. Place chicken breasts in bottom of glass baking dish and pour creamy sauce over the top.
4. Bake in the oven for 20 minutes turning halfway.
5. Slice chicken breasts into strips, place on gluten free wrap along-side lettuce

25. *Thai Lime Pork Wraps*

Prep Time: 10 mins

Ingredients:

1 lb. pork tenderloin

1 onion, sliced

2 limes, juiced

1 tsp. salt, black pepper

8 large lettuce leaves

Extra virgin olive oil

Procedures:

1. Preheat oven to 400 degrees, lightly coat a baking tray with extra virgin olive oil.
2. Slice tenderloin into 1" pieces and toss with lime juice, salt pepper.
3. Place tenderloin into the oven to cook for 30 minutes.
4. Place lettuce leaves on a flat surface, spoon a little tenderloin per lettuce leaf, top with onion slices, roll and secure with a toothpick.

26. Avocado Shrimp Wrap

Prep Time: 10 mins.

Ingredients:

1 lb. shrimp, peeled, deveined

1 red bell pepper, seeded and chopped

1 medium onion, peeled, chopped

1/2 avocado, pitted

1 lemon, juiced

1/2 tsp. salt, black pepper

4 flax tortillas

Procedures:

1. Mix shrimp with bell pepper and onion in a glass bowl.
2. Place avocado in a blender and mix until smooth, add lemon juice, salt, pepper.
3. Mix avocado into shrimp mixture and place a quarter of the mixture into each flax tortilla.

27. Chicken Lemon Cabbage Wraps

Prep Time: 10 mins.

Ingredients:

1 lb. chicken breasts, roasted

1 red bell pepper, seeded, chopped

1 celery stalk, finely chopped

1 onion, peeled and chopped

4 cloves garlic

1 lemon, juiced

1/2 head cabbage

1 tsp. salt, pepper

Procedures:

1. Heat large pot of water until boiling.
2. Separate cabbage leaves and place in boiling water for two minutes, remove and run under cold water.
3. Chop chicken breasts into ½" pieces, place in large bowl and mix with remaining ingredients save cabbage.
4. Spoon chicken mixture into cabbage leaves and secure roll with a toothpick or enjoy open faced.

28. Spinach Cheese Wrap

Prep Time: 10 min.

Ingredients:

6 cups spinach, chopped

2 tomatoes, diced

1 small onion, minced

4 cloves garlic, minced

3/4 cup cashew, soaked overnight

1 tsp. salt, black pepper

Extra virgin olive oil

4 cauliflower wraps (gluten free)

Procedures:

1. Place cashews in food processor with lemon juice and crush until crumbly.
2. Heat olive oil in skillet; add onion, garlic and sauté for a minute.
3. Add spinach, tomato and continue to sauté for two minutes.
4. Reduce heat to low, add salt, pepper and cook for another five minutes.
5. Spoon spinach into cauliflower wrap, sprinkle with cashew cheese and roll.

29. *Sausage and Pepper Wrap*

Prep Time: 10 mins.

Ingredients:

2 lean Italian sausage links

1 onion, sliced

2 red bell peppers

1 green bell pepper

4 cloves, garlic, minced

Salt and pepper to taste

Extra virgin olive oil

4 flax tortillas

Procedures:

1. Slice sausage into ½" rounds.
2. Heat 2 tbsp. olive oil in a skillet, add sausage, sauté.
3. Add bell peppers, onion, and garlic and continue to sauté until onion is golden brown.
4. Spoon sausage and peppers into flax tortilla.

30. *Sweet Potato Burrito Caramelized Onions*

Prep Time: 5 mins.

Cook time: 20 min

Ingredients:

2 sweet potatoes

1 large onion, sliced

1 red bell pepper, seeded and sliced

1/2 cup cashew, soaked overnight, crushed

1 tsp. dry mustard

2 tbsp. lemon juice

1/2 tsp. cayenne, oregano, cumin

1 tsp. salt, black pepper

Extra virgin olive oil

4 flax tortillas

Procedures:

1. Peel sweet potato, chop and place in a steamer for 20 minutes or until soft.
2. Heat 2 tbsp. olive oil in a skillet and sauté onion and bell pepper; add cashew and sauté for a minute, set aside.
3. Mash sweet potato and mix with spices.
4. Spoon a quarter of potato mixture into each wrap, top with sautéed onion, bell pepper and cashew, and roll into a burrito.

31. Paleo Style Coconut Chicken

Prep Time: 10 minutes

Cooking Time: 20 minutes

Ingredients:

450 g (1 pound) boneless and skinless chicken breasts cut into strips

60 ml (¼ cup) coconut flour

60 ml (¼ cup) shredded coconut, organic, unsweetened

0.5 ml (⅛ teaspoon) sea salt

1 egg

30 ml (2 tablespoons) coconut oil

Procedures:

1. Whisk together coconut flour, shredded coconut and salt in a medium bowl.
2. In another bowl, beat egg.
3. Dip chicken breasts strip in the egg and then into the flour mixture.
4. Heat oil in a frying pan over medium high heat.
5. Place chicken in the pan and cook until golden brown on both sides.
6. Remove from the pan and serve on a plate.

32. *Ancestral Roasted Chicken*

Prep Time: 10 minutes

Cooking Time: 20 minutes

Ingredients:

1 liter of cooking wine

1 bay leaf

4 tbsps. Orange peel, chopped coarsely

3 cloves garlic

½ tsp. thyme

½ tsp. black pepper

½ tbsp. salt

1 whole chicken

Procedures:

1. Prepare chicken by placing at room temperature for at least an hour.

2. With paper towels, pat dry chicken inside and out.

3. As you begin preparing chicken seasoning, preheat oven to 450oF.

4. In a small bowl, mix thyme, pepper and salt.

5. Get 1/3 of the seasoning and wipe inside the chicken.

6. Also place inside of the chicken the bay leaf, citrus peel and garlic.

7. Tuck the wing tips and tie chicken legs together. Spread remaining seasoning all over and around the chicken.

8. Then place on a roasting pan.

9. Pop in the oven and bake for 50-60 minutes or until chicken is a golden brown, juices run clear or chicken things or breasts register a 1600F temperature.

10. Remove from oven and let it sit for 15 minutes more before cutting up and serving the roasted chicken.

33. *Paleo Pineapple Chicken Slow Cooker Recipe*

Prep Time: 15 minutes

Cooking Time: 4-6 hours

Ingredients:

2 jars (12oz each) of clean salsa

½ fresh pineapple, chopped

8 small zucchini, shredded

4 large skinless, boneless chicken breasts

Procedures:

1. Start by washing all the zucchini, then use a food processer to shred the zucchini or use a grater to grate it.

2. Remove skin from pineapple and cut half of the pineapple into chunks for the recipe. Save the rest of the pineapple for a snack, breakfast or another recipe. Store pineapple and shredded zucchini in the refrigerator.

3. Place the chicken and the salsa in your slow cooker. Cover and cook on low for 4-6 hours or until chicken is very tender.

4. After the chicken is done cooking, use two forks to shred the chicken.

5. After shredding the chicken, mix the pineapple and the shredded zucchini into the shredded chicken.

34. *Paleo Lime, Cilantro and Chili Chicken Slow Cooker Recipe*

Prep Time: 15 minutes

Marinate Time: overnight

Cooking Time: 6 hours

Ingredients:

½ cup of fresh lime juice

1 tablespoon of olive oil

Dry rub (1 teaspoon each of pepper, sea salt and cumin and 1 tablespoon each of cayenne and chili powder)

2 handfuls of cilantro, fresh

3 garlic cloves

1 whole lime

1 large, organic, free range whole chicken (5-6 pounds)

Procedures:

1. Take the chicken out of the packaging, rinsing it in cold water. Use paper towels to blot the chicken dry.

2. Using the dry rub you made, rub the chicken with some of the rub, making sure that the entire chicken is covered with the spice mixture.

3. In a food processor or blender, add the garlic, lime juice, olive oil and cilantro. Blend until you have a thick, even consistency.

4. Take the whole lime, using a fork or knife to poke many holes in it, and then insert it into the chicken cavity.

5. In a large crock pot liner or a large zip lock bag, place the chicken. Once the chicken is securely in the bag, pour the cilantro marinade over the chicken. Ensure that the chicken is coated evenly with marinade and use fingers to work the marinade into the skin. Use a knife to puncture the break area a few times so the marinade soaks

into the meat. Seal the bag tightly and place the bag in a pot or pan to make sure you don't have any leaks. Place in the refrigerator and allow it to marinate overnight.

6. The next morning, put the chicken into a slow cooker. Any leftover marinade should also go into the slow cooker.

7. Cover and cook on low for about 6-8 hours, or until chicken is fully cooked and tender.

8. Remove chicken from the slow cooker and serve while hot. Enjoy!

35. Paleo Chicken Tikka Masala Slow Cooker Recipe

Prep Time: 20 minutes
Cooking Time: 3 hours

Ingredients:

1 cup of coconut milk

3 cloves of garlic, minced

1 teaspoon of ground coriander

1 tablespoon of coconut palm sugar

½ teaspoon of salt

2 tablespoons of ghee or grass fed butter

1 tablespoon of ginger root, minced

½ yellow onion, sliced thinly

2-3 tablespoons of coconut oil

1 teaspoon of ground cumin

¼ teaspoon of red chili flakes

2 cups of crushed tomatoes, organic

1 tablespoon of garam masala, plus 2 teaspoons

2 pounds of chicken thighs, organic

Fresh cilantro

Procedures:

1. Remove any excess skin and fat from the chicken thighs.

2. Place thighs in a large bowl, sprinkling with a tablespoon of the garam masala, making sure the chicken is evenly coated.

3. Heat two tablespoons of the coconut oil in a skillet over medium high heat.

4. Place thighs in the pan, skin side down, allowing the thighs to sear.

5. Flip and sear on the other side. Seared thighs can be added to the slow cooker. Top with the sliced onion.

6. Melt the ghee or butter in a small sauce pan, add the garlic and ginger root, cooking until it sizzles.

7. Add the crushed tomatoes and the coconut milk.

8. Place the rest of the garam masala, cumin, red chili flakes, coconut palm sugar, coriander and salt in the butter mixture.

9. Allow to simmer until the spices mix together well and it begins to pop and simmer. Remove from heat, pouring the sauce over the chicken and onions.

10. Cover the slow cooker, turn on low heat and allow to cook for three hours.

11. Thighs should be fully cooked and the onions should be tender. If the chicken needs a bit more time, cook for another hour.

12. Serve while hot alone or over cauliflower rice, topped with a bit of chopped cilantro.

36. Portuguese style Chicken

Prep Time: 30 minutes
Cooking Time: 65 minutes
Marinade time: 4-12 hours

Ingredients:

1 whole organic chicken
1 tablespoon of Piri Piri spice mix
4 garlic cloves, minced
1 onion
60 ml (¼ cup) freshly squeezed lemon juice
60 ml (¼cup) organic maple syrup
5 ml (1 teaspoon) sea salt
85 ml (⅓ cup) olive oil
30 ml (2 tablespoons) apple cider vinegar
Sea salt and fresh ground pepper to taste

Procedures:

1. Mix all the ingredients except the chickens in a food processor. Blend until you obtain a smooth marinade.
2. Place the chicken on a working surface, breast side down. With a large and sharp knife, cut open the back of the chicken so that it will flatten and open up. Turn the chicken over, and press firmly to flatten. Repeat for the second chicken.
3. In a large zip lock bag, place one chicken in with half of the marinade. Repeat with the second chicken. Refrigerate for a minimum of 4 hours and up to 12 hours.
4. Remove both chickens from the marinade, and place in a roasting oven pan. Place the chickens, breast side facing up. Season with salt and pepper to taste. Reserve the marinade.
5. Place the excess marinade in a small sauce pan, and cook on low heat for 20 minutes
6. Place the chickens on the middle rack, in pre-heated 400°F oven, and cook for 30 minutes.
7. After 30 minutes, take out the chicken, smear with some of the marinades on both sides, and cook for another 30 minutes.

8. Brush the breast side with the rest of the marinade, and broil for 5 minutes.
9. Cut the chicken into pieces, and serve with steamed vegetables of your choice.

37. *Slow-cooked Chicken Spanish style*

Prep Time: 12 minutes

Cooking Time: 4 hours

Ingredients:

8 oz. chicken legs (drumsticks)
1/3 cup fresh orange juice
2 tsp. orange zest
¼ cup raw honey
3 cloves garlic (minced)
1 tbsp. grated ginger
1 tbsp. coconut aminos
½ tbsp. balsamic vinegar
1 tsp. tomato paste
1 tbsp. sesame seeds
(Optional) ½ tbsp. Sriracha sauce(Be careful with this ingredient if your sensitive)
Green onions (chopped)
Sesame seeds

Procedures:
1. Whisk all the ingredients in a bowl (except chicken).
2. Season the chicken with salt and pepper and place in a slow cooker and pour in the sauce. Cook over low heat for 4 hours.
3. Place the chicken on a plate and put the sauce in a small pan. Simmer the sauce for 15 minutes. Pour the sauce over the chicken and garnish with green onions and sesame seeds.

38. Chicken Drumsticks Tandoori & Mango Chutney

Prep Time: 45 minutes

Cooking Time: 30 minutes

Marinade time: 4 hours

Ingredients:

16 chicken drumsticks

Tandoori mix:
250 ml (1 cup) coconut milk

Juice of 2 lemons

125 ml (½ cup) olive oil

60ml (¼ cup) tandoori spices

15 ml (1 tablespoon) red sweet paprika

Sea salt & fresh ground pepper to taste

Mango Chutney:
30 ml (2 tablespoons) olive oil

2 garlic cloves, minced

15 ml (1 tablespoon) minced fresh ginger

2 mango, peeled and cubed

30 ml (2 tablespoons) raw honey

60 ml (¼ cup) apple cider vinegar

60 ml (¼ cup) water

2 cinnamon sticks

4 cloves

1-2 pinches of crushed chilies to taste

Sea salt & fresh ground pepper to taste

Procedures:
1. Put all the ingredients for the tandoori mix together in a zip lock bag or a container, place the chicken in, and let marinate for at least 4h00.
2. For the chutney, in a small frying pan, heat the oil on high, reduce heat to medium, and cook the garlic and ginger for 2 to 3 minutes. Add all the remaining

ingredients, and cook covered for an additional 15 minutes on low heat. Remove the cover, and cook another 10 minutes or until you obtain a consistent chutney. Cool before serving

3. Pre-heat oven to 400°F.
4. Place the drumsticks on a slightly oiled baking sheet. Cook for 30 minutes until the chicken is well cooked.
5. Serve with the mango chutney and your favorite steamed vegetables.

39. *Orange Chicken Paleo Style*

Prep Time: 5 minutes

Cooking Time: 20 minutes

Ingredients:

15 ml (1 tablespoon) coconut oil

225 g (½ pound) boneless chicken breast, cut into strips

1 garlic clove, minced

125 ml (½ cup) fresh orange juice

30 ml (2 tablespoons) grated orange

Salt and pepper for seasoning

Procedures:

1. Heat oil in a large frying pan over medium heat.
2. Stir in garlic and sauté 1 minute. Add chicken strips, and cook a few minutes, stirring occasionally until chicken is not pink any more.
3. Add orange juice, cover, and continue to cook for 15 minutes over medium-low, until chicken is tender and juices almost run clear.
4. Sprinkle grated orange, season with salt and pepper, and serve.

40. *Paleo Greek Style Chicken*

Prep Time: 30 minutes

Cooking Time: 65 minutes

Marinade time: 4 hours

Ingredients:

1 whole organic chicken

½ cup olive oil

3 garlic cloves, minced

1 tablespoon chopped fresh rosemary

60 ml (¼ cup) freshly squeezed lemon juice

5 ml (1 teaspoon) thyme

1 tablespoon chopped fresh oregano

Sea salt and fresh ground pepper to taste

Procedures:

1. Mix all the ingredients except the chickens in a food processor. Blend until you obtain a smooth marinade.
2. Place the chicken on a working surface, breast side down. With a large and sharp knife, cut open the back of the chicken so that it will flatten and open up. Turn the chicken over, and press firmly to flatten. Repeat for the second chicken.
3. In a large zip lock bag, place one chicken in with half of the marinade. Repeat with the second chicken. Refrigerate for a minimum of 4 hours and up to 12 hours.
4. Remove both chickens from the marinade, and place in a roasting oven pan. Place the chickens, breast side facing up. Season with salt and pepper to taste. Reserve the marinade.
5. Place the excess marinade in a small sauce pan, and cook on low heat for 20 minutes
6. Place the chickens on the middle rack, in pre-heated 400°F oven, and cook for 30 minutes.

7. After 30 minutes, take out the chicken, smear with some of the marinade on both sides, and cook for another 30 minutes.
8. Brush the breast side with the rest of the marinade, and broil for 5 minutes.
9. Cut the chicken into pieces, and serve with steamed vegetables of your choice.

41. Paleo Greek Lemon Chicken

Prep Time: 10 minutes

Cooking Time: 50 minutes

Marinade time: 4 hours

Ingredients:

4 pounds skin-on, bone-in chicken thighs

1 tablespoon kosher salt

1 tablespoon dried oregano

1 teaspoon freshly ground black pepper

1 teaspoon dried rosemary

1 pinch cayenne pepper

1/2 cup fresh lemon juice

1/2 cup olive oil

6 cloves garlic, minced

2/3 cup chicken broth, plus splash to deglaze pan

chopped fresh oregano for garnish

Procedures:

1. Preheat oven to 425 degrees F (220 degrees C). Lightly oil a large roasting pan.
2. Place chicken pieces in large bowl. Season with salt, oregano, pepper, rosemary, and cayenne pepper. Add fresh lemon juice, olive oil, and garlic. Coat with marinade.
3. Transfer chicken pieces, skin side up, in prepared roasting pan, reserving marinade Drizzle with 2/3 cup chicken broth. Spoon remainder of marinade over chicken.
4. Place in preheated oven. Bake in the preheated oven for 20 minutes. Toss chicken, keeping chicken skin side up; continue baking until chicken is browned and cooked through, about 25 minutes more. An instant-read

thermometer inserted near the bone should read 165 degrees F (74 degrees C). Transfer chicken to serving platter and keep warm.

5. Place roasting pan on the stove over medium heat. Add a splash of broth and stir up browned bits from the bottom of the pan. Strain; spoon juices over chicken. Top with chopped oregano.

42. *Veggie Stew from Jamaica*

Prep Time: 10 minutes

Cooking Time: 10 minutes

Ingredients:

1 tbsp. cilantro, chopped

1 tsp. salt

1 tsp. pepper

1 tbsp. lime juice

2 cups collard greens, sliced

3 cups carrots cut into bite-sized chunks

½ yellow plantain, cut into bite-size pieces

1 cup okra, cut into ½" pieces

2 cups potatoes cut into bite-sized cubes

2 cups taro, cut into bite sized cubes

2 cups pumpkin, cut into bite sized cubes

2 cups water

2 cups coconut milk

2 bay leaves

3 green onions, white bottom removed

½ tsp. dried thyme

½ tsp. ground allspice

4 garlic cloves, minced

1 onion, chopped

1 tbsp. olive oil

Procedures:

1. On medium fire place a stockpot and heat oil. Sauté onions for 4 minutes or until translucent and soft.

2. Add thyme, all spice and garlic. Sauté for a minute.

3. Pour in water and coconut milk and bring to a simmer. Add bay leaves and green onions.

4. Once simmering, slow fire to keep the broth at a simmer and add taro and pumpkin.

5. Cook for 5 minutes.

6. Add potatoes and cook for three minutes.

7. Add carrots, plantain and okra. Mix and cook for five minutes.

8. Then remove and fish for thyme sprigs, bay leaves and green onions and discard.

9. Add collard greens and cook for four minutes or until bright green and darker in color.

10. Turn off fire, add pepper, salt and lime juice to taste

11. Once it tastes good, mix well, transfer to a serving bowl, serve and enjoy.

43. *Roasted Beef with Nutty Vegetables*

Prep Time: 15 minutes

Cooking Time: 35 minutes

Ingredients:

30 ml (2 tablespoons) olive oil

450 g (2 pounds) lean beef steak (brisket), sliced

30 ml (2 tablespoons) grainy Dijon Mustard

Montreal steak spice to taste

Garlic powder to taste

1 onion, sliced

15 ml (1 tablespoon) garlic, minced

250 ml (1 cup) asparagus, sliced

2 zucchinis, cubed

30 ml (2 tablespoons) almond butter

30 ml (2 tablespoons) almond slivers (optional)

Salt and pepper to taste

Procedures:

1. Preheat the oven to 160°C/325°F.
2. Heat oil in a skillet over high heat.
3. Rub each steak with mustard, Montreal steak spices, and garlic. When the skillet is hot, stir in the steak slices, and cook for 1-2 minutes on each side until beef is nicely colored.
4. Transfer beef to a baking dish, season with salt and pepper. Place in preheated oven and bake for 10-15 minutes, depending on steak thickness and how you like your steak cooked. When the steaks are cooked to your liking, remove from oven and let rest for a few minutes before serving. This will make your steak juicier.
5. While steaks are baking, in the same skillet, add some more olive oil if necessary, sauté onions and almond slivers (optional) for 2-3 minutes, stirring often. Add

asparagus and zucchini and cook 4-5 minutes until vegetables are tender but still crispy. Remove from heat, add almond butter and parsley. Serve each steak with a generous portion of the nutty vegetables

44. Paleo Sausage Delight

Prep Time: 15 minutes

Cooking Time: 25 minutes

Ingredients:

6 Paleo-approved sausages of your choice

60 ml (¼ cup) olive oil

60 ml (¼ cup) apple cider vinegar

20 white mushrooms, trimmed

¼ cup fresh flat parsley, minced

2 sweet peppers, sliced into 1 inch strips

2 red onions, sliced into ½ inch strips

Sea salt and fresh ground pepper to taste

Procedures:

1. Pre-heat the oven to 200°C/400°F.
2. In a large mixing bowl, combine all ingredients except parsley. Season with salt and freshly ground pepper to taste.
3. Lay the sausages and vegetable mix on a parchment paper-covered baking sheet, and cook for 40 minutes.
4. Sprinkle with parsley and serve with your favorite mustard and a side of slaw.

45. Pork Chops with Apple

Prep Time: 10 minutes

Cooking Time: 20 minutes

Ingredients:

15 ml (1 tablespoon) coconut oil

2 pork chops

1 large onion, sliced

2 apples, sliced

Salt and freshly ground black pepper to taste

Procedures:

1. Heat oil in a large pan.
2. Put chops in the pan, and cook for 5 minutes on each side until golden browned.
3. Add onion and apples, and continue to cook for 7 to 9 minutes until the onion and apples are tender.
4. Sprinkle with salt and pepper and serve.

46. Paleo Spicy Chipotle Beef Brisket Slow Cooker Recipe

Prep Time: 7 minutes

Cooking Time: 8 Hours

Ingredients:

2 cups of beef stock

1 tablespoon of apple cider vinegar

½-1 cup of Chipotle adobo sauce

3 cloves of fresh garlic

½ teaspoon of ground cloves

2 bay leaves

1 white onion, chopped

2 teaspoons of oregano

1 beef brisket, 3-4 pounds

Procedures:

1 In a food processor or a blender, combine the beef stock, apple cider vinegar, adobo sauce, garlic, ground cloves, onion and oregano. Process until you have a liquid puree.

2 Take about ¼ of the puree, placing it in the bottom of the slow cooker.

3 Add the bay leaves to the bottom of the slow cooker.

4 Trim excessive fat off the beef brisket, then place in the slow cooker, placing the fat side on the bottom. Leave only a little fat.

5 Take the rest of the puree, pouring over the beef brisket, ensuring that the sides and top are well coated.

6 Turn the slow cooker on low, cooking it for 8 hours.

7 When it is done cooking, remove the beef brisket from the slow cooker, using two forks to shred the brisket.

8 Place shredded meat in a bowl, then pour some of the leftover liquid from the slow cooker over the meat to ensure it stays nice and moist.

9 Serve the brisket in lettuce wraps, over a salad or in strips with vegetable side dishes. Enjoy while warm.

47. Paleo Asian Inspired Pepper Steak Slow Cooker Recipe

Prep Time: 7 minutes

Cooking Time: 6 Hours

Ingredients:

¼ cup of tamari (wheat free)
2 tablespoons of coconut oil
1 green bell pepper, cut into thin strips
2 cloves of garlic, minced
1 onion, cut into slices
1 can of diced tomatoes (16oz)
1 can of bean sprouts (16oz), drained
2 lbs of sirloin steak
Pepper and salt to taste

Procedures:

1 Place the steak on a chopping board, cutting it into ½ inch strips, cutting at an angle.

2 Heat the oil in a large frying pan, place the sliced steak into the pan, allowing to cook until it becomes lightly browned.

3 Drain away any fat and coat the steak with freshly ground black pepper.

4 Place the steak in the slow cooker.

5 Add the tamari and the minced garlic. Mix until the steak is coated with the garlic and tamari.

6 Cover the slow cooker and turn on low. Allow to cook for about 6 hours.

7   An hour before you want to serve the pepper steak, add the green peppers, onions, tomatoes and sprouts.

8   Turn crock pot on high and cook for another hour. Serve while hot and eat immediately. Enjoy!

48. *Paleo Sweet and Spicy Slow Cooker Carnitas*

Prep Time: 7 minutes

Cooking Time: 8 Hours

Ingredients:

2 teaspoons of lime juice

2 tablespoons of orange juice

1 tablespoon of honey or agave

1 ½ cups of diced tomatoes

¼ cup of green chilies, diced

1 teaspoon of fresh garlic, minced

¼ cup of yellow onion, diced

½ cup of barbecue sauce

½ teaspoon of salt

1 tablespoon of cumin

1 teaspoon of garlic powder

2 teaspoons of chili powder

2 teaspoons of onion powder

2-3 pounds of pork shoulder or butt roast

4-6 lettuce bowls

Procedures:

1. Place the pork roast in the slow cooker. Top with the chilies, onions, minced garlic and diced tomatoes.

2. In a small bowl, mix together the orange juice, lime juice and honey/agave. Combine until well mixed.

3. Add the cumin, chili powder, salt, onion powder, garlic powder and barbecue sauce to the juice mixture. Mix well.

4. Pour the juice mixture over the pork roast and veggies.

5. Cover and turn the slow cooker on low, cook for 6-8 hours.

6. An hour before serving, use a fork to shred the pork, then stir all the ingredients together again to mix up the flavors. Allow to cook for another hour.

7. Serve the shredded pork carnitas in lettuce bowls. Top with guacamole, diced, fresh tomatoes, a bit of cilantro and any other toppings you desire. Enjoy immediately.

49. *Paleo Meatballs and Spaghetti Squash Slow Cooker Recipe*

Prep Time: 7 minutes

Cooking Time: 5 Hours

Ingredients:

1 lb of paleo friendly, ground Italian sausage
4-6 whole cloves of garlic
1 spaghetti squash
2 tablespoons of olive oil
2 teaspoons of Italian seasoning
1 14oz can of tomato sauce
2 tablespoons of hot pepper relish
Parsley (for garnishing, if desired)

Procedures:

1. Place the olive oil, hot pepper relish, tomato sauce, Italian seasoning and garlic in the slow cooker. Stir together until well combined.

2. Wash the spaghetti squash well and then cut it in half. Remove all of the seeds from the squash. Place the halves face down on top of the sauce in the slow cooker.

3. Take ground Italian sausage and roll into small meatballs. Place the meatballs around the spaghetti squash.

4. Cover the slow cooker and cook for about five hours on low.

5. Remove the spaghetti squash from the slow cooker, using a fork to pull out all the spaghetti from the squash.

6. Put spaghetti squash on plates and then serve with the sauce and the Italian sausage meatballs.

7. Garnish with a bit of parsley on the side if desired. Enjoy while hot.

50. Nutty Tilapia Fillets

Prep Time: 15 minutes

Cooking Time: 10 minutes

Ingredients:

4 large Tilapia fillets

15 ml (1 tablespoon) black peppercorn

8 ml (½ tablespoon) fennel seeds

8 ml (½ tablespoon) smoked paprika

45 ml (3 tablespoons) coconut butter or grass fed butter

125 ml (½ cup) of pecan

15 ml (1 tablespoon) fresh chopped flat leave parsley

Sea salt & fresh ground pepper to taste

1 lemon, sliced

Procedures:

1. Using a pestle and mortar, crush and grind together peppercorn, fennel seeds and paprika
2. Season both sides of the tilapia with the spices.
3. Using a frying pan, melt 2 tablespoons of the butter over medium heat. Add the fillets, and cook for 4 minutes, turn the tilapia over and cook for an additional 3 to 4 minutes until the fish is done.
4. Place your cooked fillets on a warm serving plate, and reserve.
5. In the same hot frying pan, add the rest of the butter and the pecans. Cook for about 1 minute. Add some lemon juice to taste, and mix well.
6. Place the lemony nuts on the fillets, sprinkle with the parsley, and serve with your favorite side vegetables and lemon slices.

51. Tilapia with Thai Curry

Prep Time: 10 minutes

Cooking Time: 25 minutes

Ingredients:

125 ml (½ cup) coconut milk

250 ml (1 cup) fresh basil leaves

60 ml (4 tablespoons) Thai curry paste

30 ml (2 tablespoons) olive oil

2 tilapia fillets

1 large red bell peppers, deseeded, julienne

1 onion, sliced

60 ml (¼ cup) scallions, sliced

30 ml (2 tablespoons) fish sauce*

Salt and freshly ground black pepper to taste

Procedures:

1. Place coconut milk, basil leaves, and Thai curry paste into a food processor and blend until smooth.
2. Heat oil in a large pan. Add tilapia fillets, and cook for 5 minutes on each side until little browned. Remove tilapia to a plate, and set aside.
3. Add red bell peppers, onion, and scallions in the same pan, and cook until the vegetables are tender.
4. Add coconut milk mixture, and cook for 5 minutes until thickens. Add in reserved fish fillets; simmer until tilapia is heated through.

5. Drizzle fish sauce, season with salt and pepper and serve.

* Make sure that the fish sauce is completely paleo, containing fish and salt only. It is suggested to read the label before purchasing.

52. *Stuffed Sea Bass*

Prep Time: 15 minutes

Cooking Time: 25 minutes

Ingredients:

4 sea bass, about 350 to 450 grams (¾ to 1 pound) each, cleaned, head removed

125 ml (½ cup) olive oil

45 ml (3 tablespoons) olive oil

225 g (½ pound) white mushrooms, sliced

1 tablespoon fresh parsley, minced

1 green pepper, diced

Freshly squeezed lemon juice to taste

Sea salt and fresh ground pepper to taste

Procedures:

1. Pre-heat the oven to 305°C/425°F.
2. Salt and pepper the inside of the bass. Add lemon juice to taste.
3. Place each fish on a foil sheet large enough to cover the fish.
4. Melt half of the butter in a medium size frying pan, add the shallots, and cook 2-3 minutes. Add the mushroom, pepper, and parsley. Season with salt and pepper to taste, and cook for an additional 6 minutes until vegetables are tender.
5. Stuff each fish with ¼ of the vegetable mix, and brush the fish with olive oil. Seal the aluminum foil well. Place the foil packets on a baking sheet. Cook for 16 minutes.
6. Take out of the oven and make sure the fish is well cooked. If not, bake for an additional 2 minutes or until cooked.
7. Serve with lemon slices and your favorite vegetables.

53. Creamy Salmon Bake

Prep Time: 10 minutes

Cooking Time: 10 minutes

Ingredients:

Pepper and salt to taste

¼ tsp. garlic powder

1 tbsp. minced fresh dill

¼ cup Mayo

2 salmon filets, around 6-oz each

Procedures:

1. Grease a baking sheet and preheat oven to 450oF.

2. Mix pepper, salt, garlic powder, dill and mayo in a medium bowl.

3. Spread ½ of mayo mixture onto one filet and the other half to the second filet.

4. Place on prepped baking sheet, pop into the oven and bake for 7 minutes or until flaky and cooked.

5. Remove from oven and serve.

54. *Lime and Coconut Shrimp Thai Style*

Prep Time: 5 minutes
Cooking Time: 10 minutes

Ingredients:

1 tbsp. lime juice

1 tbsp. oil

1 garlic clove, sliced thinly

½ tsp. black pepper

½ tsp. salt

½ tsp. sriracha

1 tsp. cayenne pepper

3 tbsps. Yellow curry powder

1 cup unsweetened shredded coconut

1/3 cup coconut flour

3 egg whites, whisked

1 6-oz can coconut milk

1 lb. shrimp, peeled and deveined

Procedures:

1. In a small bowl, whisk egg whites until foamy.

2. In a second bowl, place shredded coconut.

3. The third bowl, mix pepper, salt, cayenne, 2 tbsps. Curry powder and coconut flour.

4. Dip shrimp in bowl #1, then bowl #3, then bowl #2. Repeat process for all shrimp and arrange them on a plate in one layer.

5. Once done, heat a large nonstick saucepan on medium fire and add garlic and oil. Cook for 3 minutes.

6. Add 1 tbsp. curry powder, sriracha and coconut milk. Cook for a minute or until bubbly.

7. Add shrimps and cook for 3 minutes or until tails curl and are cooked.

8. Remove from pan, transfer to a serving plate and add lime juice before serving.

55. *Peas and Ham Thick Soup*

Prep Time: 10 minutes

Cooking Time: 25 minutes

Ingredients:

Pepper and salt to taste

1 lb. ham, coarsely chopped

24 oz. frozen sweet peas

4 cup ham stock

¼ cup white wine

1 carrot, chopped coarsely

1 onion, chopped coarsely

2 tbsps. butter, divided

Procedures:

1. On medium fire place a medium pot and heat oil.
2. Sauté for 6 minutes the onion or until soft and translucent.
3. Add wine and cook for 4 minutes or until nearly evaporated.
4. Add ham stock and bring to a simmer and simmer continuously while covered for 4 minutes.
5. Add peas and cook for 7 minutes or until tender.
6. Meanwhile, in a nonstick fry pan, cook to a browned crisp the ham in 1 tbsp. butter, around 6 minutes.
7. Remove from fire and set aside.

8. When peas are soft, transfer to a blender and puree.

9. Return to pot; continue cooking while seasoning with pepper, salt and ½ of crisped ham.

10. Once soup is to your desire taste, turn off the fire.

11. Transfer to 4 serving bowls and garnish evenly with crisped ham.

56. Chicken Bacon Crock Pot Chowder

Prep time: 20 minutes

Cook time: 8 hours

Ingredients:

Thyme (1 teaspoon, dried)

Garlic cloves (4, minced)

Garlic powder (1 teaspoon)

Shallot (1, chopped)

Black pepper (1 teaspoon)

Leek (1, sliced)

Salt (1 teaspoon)

Celery (2, diced)

Bacon (1 lb, cooked and crumbled)

Cremini mushrooms (6 ounces, sliced)

Heavy cream (1 cup)

Onion (1, sliced)

Cream cheese (8 ounces)

Butter (4 tablespoons, divided)

Chicken breasts (1 lb)

Chicken stock (2 cups, divided)

Procedures:

1. Turn your slow cooker on to low
2. Throw in the vegetables, stock, salt, and pepper. Cook for an hour
3. Sear the chicken in a skillet with the last of the butter this will be about five minutes
1. Remove from pan and deglaze with last of the chicken stock

4. Dump the chicken stock into the cock pot
5. Add in heavy cream, cream cheese, thyme, garlic powder. Stir
6. After the chicken is no longer hot, cub and throw in the slow cooker.
7. Stir until all ingredients are mixed together
8. Cover and cook for 6 hours

57. Special Paleo Soup

Preparation time: 15 minutes

Cooking time: 40 minutes

Ingredients:

1 yellow onion, finely chopped
1 tablespoon ghee
3 thyme springs, chopped
3 garlic cloves, finely minced
28 ounces canned tomatoes, chopped
6 ounces tomato paste
¼ cup water
1 pound sausage, chopped
14 ounces beef stock
6 mushrooms, chopped
1 small red bell pepper, chopped
5 ounces pepperoni
2.5 ounces black olives, chopped
A pinch of red pepper flakes

Procedures:

1. Heat up a pot with the ghee over medium high heat and melt it.
2. Add half of the onion, garlic, and thyme, stir and cook for 5 minutes.
3. Add tomatoes, tomato paste and water, stir, bring to a boil, reduce heat to medium-low and simmer for 20 minutes.
4. Pour this into your blender, pulse well and leave aside for now.
5. Heat up a pot over medium-high heat, add sausage, stir and cook for a few minutes, breaking into small pieces with a fork.
6. Add the rest of the onion, mushrooms and the bell pepper, stir and cook for 5 minutes.
7. Add tomato soup you've blended and beef stock, stir and cook for 5 more minutes.
8. Heat up a pan over medium high heat, add pepperoni slices, stir and cook until they brown.
9. Pour soup into bowls, top with red pepper flakes, olives, and pepperoni. Enjoy!

58. Tomato and Basil Soup

Preparation time: 10 minutes

Cooking time: 35 minutes

Ingredients:

56 ounces canned tomatoes, crushed
2 cups tomato juice
2 cups chicken stock
¼ pound butter
14 basil leaves, torn
1 cup coconut milk
Salt and black pepper to the taste

Procedures:

1. Put tomatoes, tomato juice and stock in a pot, heat up over medium-high heat, bring to a boil, reduce heat, stir and simmer for 30 minutes.
2. Pour this into your blender, add basil, pulse very well and return to pot.
3. Heat up soup again, add butter and coconut milk, stir and cook on low heat for a few more minutes.
4. Add salt and pepper to the taste, stir well, pour into soup bowls and serve. Enjoy!

59. Paleo Chicken Soup

Preparation time: 15 minutes

Cooking time: 60 minutes

Ingredients:

2 teaspoons coconut oil

3 carrots, chopped

1 yellow onion, chopped

1 zucchini, chopped

12 ounces canned mushrooms, chopped

¼ butternut squash, cubed

4 cups chicken meat, already cooked and shredded

2 teaspoons rosemary, dried

1 teaspoon thyme, dried

1 tablespoon apple cider vinegar

1 teaspoon cumin

2 and ½ cups chicken stock

Salt and black pepper to the taste

Procedures:

1. Heat up a pot with the coconut oil over medium heat, add carrots and onion, stir and cook for 5 minutes.
2. Add zucchini, mushrooms, and squash, stir and cook for 5 more minutes.
3. Add chicken meat, rosemary, thyme, vinegar, cumin and chicken stock, stir, bring to a boil, reduce heat to medium-low and simmer for 40 minutes.
4. Add salt and pepper to the taste, stir again, take off heat and pour into soup bowls.

60. Delicious Cauliflower Soup

Preparation time: 10 minutes

Cooking time: 60 minutes

Ingredients:

1 yellow onion, finely chopped
2 tablespoons extra virgin olive oil
2 pounds cauliflower florets
Salt and black pepper to the taste
20 saffron threads
2 garlic cloves, minced
5 cups veggie stock

Procedures:

1. Heat up a pot with the oil over medium heat, add onion and garlic, stir and cook for 10 minutes.
2. Add cauliflower, salt and pepper to the taste, stir and cook for 12 more minutes.
3. Add stock, stir, bring to a boil, reduce heat to medium and simmer for 25 minutes.
4. Take soup off the heat, add saffron, cover pot and leave it aside for 20 minutes.
5. Transfer soup to your blender and pulse very well. Pour into soup bowls and serve right away.

61. Paleo Beef Soup

Preparation time: 10 minutes

Cooking time: 1 hour

Ingredients:

1 pound beef, ground
1 pound sausage, sliced
4 cups beef stock
30 ounces canned tomatoes, diced
1 green bell pepper, chopped
3 zucchinis, chopped
1 cup celery, chopped
1 teaspoon Italian seasoning
½ yellow onion, chopped
½ teaspoon oregano, dried
½ teaspoon basil, dried
¼ teaspoon garlic powder
Salt and black pepper to the taste

Procedures:

1. Heat up a pot over medium heat, add sausage and beef, stir, cook until it browns and drains excess fat.
2. Add tomatoes, zucchini, bell pepper, celery, onion, Italian seasoning, basil, oregano, garlic powder, salt, pepper to the taste and the stock, stir, bring to a boil, reduce heat to medium-low and simmer for 1 hour.
3. Pour into soup bowls and

62. *Root Paleo Soup*

Preparation time: 10 minutes

Cooking time: 1 hour and 30 minutes

Ingredients:

1 sweet onion, chopped
2 tablespoons butter
5 carrots, chopped
3 parsnips, chopped
3 beets, chopped
3 bacon slices
1-quart chicken stock
Salt and black pepper to the taste
2 quarts water
½ teaspoon chili flakes
1 tablespoons mixed thyme and rosemary

Procedures:

1. Heat up a Dutch oven with the butter over medium-high heat, add onion, stir and cook for 5 minutes.
2. Add carrots, parsnips, beets, bacon, chicken stock and water and stir.
3. Also add salt, pepper to the taste, chili flakes, thyme, and rosemary, stir again, bring to a boil, reduce heat to medium-low and simmer for 1 hour and 30 minutes.
4. Pour into soup bowls and serve hot.

63. *Delightful Chicken Soup*

Preparation time: 15 minutes

Cooking time: 30 minutes

Ingredients:

2 celery stalks, chopped
½ cup coconut oil
2 carrots, chopped
½ cup arrowroot
6 cups chicken stock
1 teaspoon dry parsley
½ cup water
1 bay leaf
Salt and black pepper to the taste
½ teaspoon dry thyme
1 and ½ cups coconut milk
3 cups chicken meat, already cooked and cubed

Procedures:

1. Heat up a soup pot with the oil over medium-high heat, add carrots and celery, stir and cook for 10 minutes.
2. Add stock, stir and bring to a boil.
3. In a bowl, mix arrowroot with ½ cup water and whisk well.
4. Add this to soup and also add parsley, salt, and pepper to the taste, bay leaf and thyme.
5. Stir and cook everything for 15 minutes.
6. Add chicken meat and coconut milk, stir, cook 1 more minute, take off heat, pour into soup bowls and serve.

64. *Paleo Lemon and Garlic Soup*

Preparation time: 10 minutes

Cooking time: 10 minutes

Ingredients:

- 6 cups shellfish stock
- 1 tablespoons garlic, finely minced
- 1 tablespoon ghee
- 2 eggs
- ½ cup lemon juice
- Salt and white pepper to the taste
- 1 tablespoon arrowroot powder
- Cilantro, finely chopped for serving

Procedures:

1. Heat up a pot with the ghee over medium high heat, add garlic, stir and cook for 2 minutes.
2. Add stock but reserve ½ cup, stir and bring to a simmer.
3. Meanwhile, in a bowl, mix eggs with salt, pepper, reserved stock, lemon juice and arrowroot and whisk very well.
4. Pour this into soup, stir and cook for a few minutes.
5. Ladle into bowls and serve with chopped cilantro on top.

65. Rich Paleo Soup

Preparation time: 10 minutes

Cooking time: 0

Ingredients:

1 avocado, pitted and chopped
1 cucumber, chopped
2 bunches spinach
1 and ½ cups watermelon, chopped
1 bunch cilantro, roughly chopped
Juice from 2 lemons
½ cup coconut amino
½ cup lime juice

Procedures:

1. In your kitchen blender, mix cucumber with avocado and pulse well.
2. Add cilantro, spinach, and watermelon and blend again well.
3. Add lemon and lime juice and coconut amino and pulse a few more times.
4. Transfer to soup bowls and enjoy!

66. Paleo Veggie Soup

Preparation time: 10 minutes

Cooking time: 45 minutes

Ingredients:

2 sweet potatoes, peeled and chopped
2 yellow onions, cut into eighths
2 pounds carrots, diced
4 tablespoons coconut oil
1 head garlic, cloves peeled
Salt and black pepper to the taste
2 cups chicken stock
3 tablespoons maple syrup

Procedures:

1. Put onions, carrots, sweet potatoes and garlic in a baking dish, add coconut oil, salt, and pepper to the taste, toss to coat, introduce in the oven at 425 degrees F and bake for 35 minutes.
2. Take veggies out of the oven, transfer to a pot, add chicken stock and heat everything up on the stove on medium-high heat.
3. Bring soup to a boil, reduce heat to medium, cover and simmer for 10 minutes.
4. Transfer soup to your blender, add more salt and pepper and the maple syrup, pulse well to obtain a cream, pour into soup bowls and serve.

67. *Emerald City Soup*

Prep time: 15 minutes

Cook time: none

Ingredients:

Coconut aminos (1/2 cup)
Cucumber (1)

Lime juice (1/2 cup)

Avocado (1)

Lemons (2, juiced)

Cilantro (1 bunch)

Honeydew or watermelon (1 ½ cups)

Spinach (2 bunches)

Procedures:

1. Place all the food into your food processor
2. Once smooth, place in the fridge or serve as is

68. Pumpkin and Chorizo Soup

Prep time: 10 minutes

Cook time: 25 minutes

Ingredients:

Cilantro (chopped)

Olive oil (1 tablespoon)

Salt and pepper (to taste)

Onion (1, diced)

Chorizo sausage (1/2 lb, ground)

Garlic cloves (4, minced)

Chicken broth (3 cups)

Marjoram (1 teaspoon, dried)

Pumpkin puree (30 ounces)

Oregano (1 teaspoon, dried)

Cumin (1/2 teaspoons)

Procedures:

1. Put the olive oil in a skillet
2. Sauté the onions
3. Mix in the garlic and other spices. Cook for thirty seconds
2. Dump in broth and puree. Simmer for twenty minutes covered
4. Sauté the chorizo
5. Blend soup together in the blender
6. Place back in skillet and mix in sausage
7. Enjoy with a little bit of cilantro

69. *Orange Ginger Squash Soup*

Prep time: 10 minutes

Cook time: 1 hour

Ingredients:

Almonds (sliced, optional)

Pomegranate seeds (optional)

Acorn squash (1)

Cayenne pepper (a pinch)

Olive oil (1/2 teaspoons)

Coconut aminos (1 tablespoon)

Salt and pepper (to taste)

Ginger (3/4 teaspoons, ground)

Chicken stock (2 cups)

Orange zest (1 teaspoon)

Coconut milk (1/4 cup)

Orange juice (1/4 cup, fresh)

Procedures:

1. Heat your oven to 400F
2. Slice the squash in half and remove seeds and pulp
3. Cover with olive oil and sprinkle with salt and pepper
3. Put on a pan and roast until tender. This could take about an hour.
4. As soon as the squash cools down, remove it from the flesh and put it in a sauce pan or blender.
5. Toss in the remaining ingredients
6. Blend until it is completely smooth
7. Cook until hot

8. Serve with almonds or pomegranate seeds

70. Purple Sweet Potato Soup

Prep time: 5 minutes

Cook time: 40 minutes

Ingredients:

Coconut milk (1/4 cup)

Ghee (1/2 tablespoons)

Salt (to taste)

Onion (1/2)

Vegetable broth (4 cups)

Purple sweet onion (1 ½ lb)

Procedures:

1. Melt the ghee
2. Cut up the onion and place it in the pot and allow to soften
3. Peel the skin off the sweet potato and dice it
4. Throw into the pot and stir to coat with the melted ghee
4. Dump in broth and boil
5. Lower heat and simmer for thirty-five minutes
6. Take off the heat and blend until smooth mixture
7. Salt and enjoy

71. Creamy Coconut Green Chili Chicken Soup

Prep time: 8 minutes

Cook time: 5 hours

Ingredients:

Lime (1)

Chicken breasts (2 lbs, chopped)

Cilantro (small bunch)

Carrots (6, chopped)

Coconut milk (1 cup)

Onion (1, diced)

Coconut flour (3 tablespoons)

Green chili (1 cup, diced)

Pepper (1/4 teaspoons)

Chicken stock (1 quarts)

Coriander powder (1/2 teaspoons)

Garlic (1 teaspoon, granulated)

Cumin powder (1/2 teaspoons)

Salt (1 teaspoon)

Procedures:

1. Cut up the chicken and put it into your crock pot
2. Do the same with your onion and your carrot
3. Now add in the chili, stock and seasonings
5. Stir until everything is mixed together thoroughly
4. Cook for five hours with the lid on
5. Ten minutes before it is done, mix in the coconut milk and the flour. The flour is going to cause the soup to thicken
6. Salt to taste

7. Serve with some lime juice or cilantro

72. Thai Coconut Turkey Soup

Prep time: 10 minutes

Cook time: 15 minutes

Ingredients:

Sriracha sauce (optional)

Oil (a splash)

Salt (to taste)

Onion (1, sliced)
sprouts (2 handfuls)

Shiitake mushrooms (handful, chopped)

Bell pepper (1, any color)

Garlic cloves (3, minced)

Soy sauce (1 tablespoon)

Ginger (1, julienned)

Thai curry paste (1 ½ tablespoons. green)

Cherry tomatoes (handful)

Coconut milk (1/2 cup)

Turkey stock (4 cups)

Turkey (1 cup, cooked)

Procedures:

1. Put the oil in a pan and heat
2. Drop in the onion and allow to cook until it becomes soft
3. Now add in the mushrooms and cook for five minutes
6. Lastly toss in the garlic, ginger, and tomatoes
4. Now add in your meat, stock, milk and soy sauce along with the curry paste
5. Allow boiling before reducing and simmering for two minutes
6. Take off the heat and add the bell pepper and sprouts

7. Season if you need to
8. Put in a bowl and add in cilantro and sriracha if you want

73. Carrot Soup

Prep Time: 15 minutes

Cooking Time: 30 minutes

Ingredients:

30 ml (2 tablespoons) coconut oil

2 bay leaves

1 onion, sliced

4 garlic cloves, minced

250 ml (1 cup) carrots, chopped

2 turnips, chopped

2 sweet potatoes, cubed

1 ml (¼ teaspoon) dried thyme

1000 ml (4 cups) chicken broth

30 ml (2 tablespoons) fresh chives, chopped

Sea salt and freshly ground pepper to taste

Procedures:
1. Heat oil in a large soup pan.
2. Stir in bay leaves, onion, and garlic, and sauté for few minutes until fragrant and tender.
3. Add carrots, turnips, sweet potatoes, and dried thyme, and continue to cook until the vegetables are tender.
4. Add broth and bring to boil. Cover and cook for 15 to 20 minutes.
5. Discard bay leaves. Pour soup into a food processor and pulse until smooth.
6. Season with salt and pepper.
7. Return to soup pan and let it simmer for 5 minutes.
8. Put soup in a bowl, sprinkle with chives, and serve hot.

74. Asparagus Salad

Prep time: 10 minutes

Cook time: none

Ingredients:

Olive oil (3 tablespoons)

Garlic powder (.5 teaspoons)

Onion (6, green, diced)

Tomatoes (2 cups)

Bacon (10 slices, cooked and crumbled)

Sea salt (1/8 teaspoons)

Asparagus (1.5 lbs, cut off the ends)

Procedures:

1. Steam your asparagus but make sure that it still has some crunch
2. Crumble the bacon into tomatoes, green onions and garlic powder
3. Mix with olive oil
7. Cut the asparagus into pieces into your mixture
4. Season to taste
5. Place in the fridge until chilled

75. Paleo Roasted Broccoli Salad

Prep time: 5 minutes

Cook time: 25 minutes

Ingredients:

Onion (1, halved, sliced)

Broccoli (4 cups, cut into small pieces)

Oregano (1 teaspoon)

Cherry tomatoes (2 cups)

Balsamic vinegar (1 tablespoon)

Coconut oil (1 tablespoon)

Onion (4, green, chopped)

Garlic cloves (2, minced)

Procedures:

1. Turn your oven on to 375 F
2. Put the oil, garlic, onion, tomato, and broccoli in a bowl and coat
3. Spread out on a baking sheet and cook for twenty-five minutes
8. Put back in a bowl and put the rest of the ingredients in
4. Stir and enjoy

76. Paleo Fennel Apple Slaw

Prep time: 20 minutes

Cook time: none

Ingredients:

Salt and pepper to taste

Apples (2, sliced)

Dijon mustard (1 teaspoon)

Fennel bulb (1)

Honey (1 tablespoon)

Onion (1, sliced)

Coconut oil (2 tablespoons)

Pecans (2 tablespoons, chopped, toasted)

Balsamic vinegar (2 tablespoons)

Celery seed (1 ½ teaspoons)

Salt (to taste)

Tarragon (1 tablespoon, fresh, chopped)

Procedures:

1. Put the apples, fennel, onion, celery seed, salt, tarragon, and pecans in a bowl
2. In another bowl combine the liquid ingredients
3. Season to taste
9. Drizzle over the apple mix until thoroughly incorporated into the salad
4. Season again if you want
5. Chill for 2 hours

77. Paleo Apple, Pear, and Walnut Salad

Prep time: 5 minutes

Cook time: none

Ingredients:

Walnuts (1/2 cup)

Apples (2, diced, peeled)

Cinnamon (1/2 teaspoons)

Pears (2, diced, peeled)

Raisins (1/3 cup)

Orange juice (1/3 cup)

Procedures:

1. Mix everything together
2. Put in the fridge for an hour

78. Paleo Mexican Chopped Salad

Prep time: 5 minutes

Cook time: none

Ingredients:

Chili powder (3/4 teaspoons)

Romaine lettuce (3 cups, shredded)

Olive oil (1/2 cup)

Red cabbage (2 cups, shredded)

Honey (1 tablespoon)

Tomato (1 cup, diced)

Sea salt (1 ½ teaspoons)

Jicama (1 cup)

Apple cider vinegar (3 tablespoons)

Onion (1/2 cup, diced)

Orange juice (3 tablespoons)

Cucumber (2 cups, diced)

Sunflower seeds (1/2 cup, toasted)

Avocado (1, cubed)

Cilantro (1/2 cup, chopped)

Procedures:

1. Shred your lettuce and cabbage
2. Put into a bowl
3. Dice your other vegetables
4. Mix your dressing ingredients together (if you make it yourself)
5. Drizzle in dressing
6. Serve with sunflower seeds on top

79. *Paleo Butternut Squash and Spinach Salad*

Prep time: 10 minutes

Cook time: 30 minutes

Ingredients:

Balsamic vinegar (1 cup)

Butternut squash (1, chopped)

Raisins (1 tablespoon)

Coconut oil (3 tablespoons)

Cranberries (2 tablespoons, dried)

Sea salt (1/2 teaspoons)

Shallots (2 tablespoons, chopped)

Black pepper (1/4 teaspoons)

Spinach (5 ounces)

Procedures:

1. Mix the squash, oil, salt, and pepper together in a bowl
2. Spread out over a baking sheet
3. Cook for thirty minutes at 375 F or until the squash is turning brown
4. Put the spinach in a bowl
5. Dump in the shallots, cranberries, raisins, and squash
6. Drizzle with vinegar

80. Salmon, Spinach & Apple Salad

Prep Time: 15 minutes

Cooking Time: 30 minutes

Ingredients:

225 g (½ pound) salmon fillets

For salad:
250 ml (1 cup) baby spinach

125 ml (½ cup) lettuce

125 ml (½ cup) cabbage, shredded

1 tart apple such as Granny Smith, sliced

For dressing:
30 ml (2 tablespoons) olive oil

30 ml (2 tablespoons) apple cider vinegar

1 large shallot, minced

Salt and black pepper, to taste

Procedures:
1. Preheat the oven to 180°C/350° F.
2. Place salmon fillet in a baking dish. Season with salt and pepper.
3. Add some water to cover fish. Cover with foil.
4. Bake for 10 minutes. Remove from oven and set aside.
5. In a large bowl, add salad ingredients and mix.
6. In another bowl, add all dressing ingredients and whisk till well combined.
7. Pour dressing over salad and toss to coat.
8. Serve salad with baked fish fillets.

81. The Big Salad

Prep Time: 20 minutes

Cooking Time: 0 minute

Ingredients

For Salad:
300 grams (2 cups) cooked chicken breast, chopped

2 liters (8 cups) spring mix lettuce

1 English cucumber, diced

12 cherry tomatoes

1 avocado, diced

60 ml (¼ cup) dry unsweetened cranberries

60 ml (¼ cup) chopped raw pecans or any favorite nuts

Sea salt and freshly ground pepper to taste

For Dressing:
1 cup extra virgin, cold press olive oil

60 ml (¼ cup) red wine vinegar

15 ml (1 tablespoon) Dijon mustard

30 ml (2 tablespoons) raw honey

60 ml (¼ cup) fresh basil leaves

Procedures:
1. Blend together until smooth all the ingredient of the dressing
2. In a large salad bowl, place all the salad ingredients, season with salt and pepper to taste, add some dressing to taste and mix well.

82. *Parsley and Pear Smoothie*

Preparation time: 5 minutes

Cooking time: 0

Ingredients:

1 apple pear, chopped

1 bunch parsley, roughly chopped

1 small avocado, stoned and peeled

1 pear, peeled and chopped

1 green apple, chopped

1 Granny Smith apple, chopped

6 bananas, peeled and roughly chopped

2 plums, stoned

1 cup ice

1 cup water

Procedures:

1. In your kitchen blender, mix parsley with avocado, apple pear, pear, green apple, Granny Smith apple, plums and bananas and blend very well.
2. Add ice and water and blend again very well.
3. Transfer to tall glasses and serve right away.

83. *Paleo Peach and Coconut Smoothie*

Preparation time: 5 minutes

Cooking time: 0

Ingredients:

1 cup ice
2 peaches, peeled and chopped
Lemon zest to the taste
1 cup cold coconut milk
1 drop lemon essential oil

Procedures:

1. In your kitchen blender, mix coconut milk with ice and peaches and pulse a few times.
2. Add lemon zest to the taste and 1 drop lemon essential oil and pulse a few more time.
3. Pour into glasses and serve right away.

84. Grapes & Watermelon Smoothie

Preparation time: 5 minutes

Cooking time: 0

Ingredients:

2 cups watermelon

1 cup grapes

1 banana

Procedures:

1. Prepare ingredients and place into a blender. Blend together while adding preferred liquid until desired consistency is reached.

85. Blueberry Pear Smoothie

Preparation time: 5 minutes

Cooking time: 0

Ingredients:

2 cups watermelon

2 pears

2 cups blueberries

Procedures:

1. Prepare ingredients and place into a blender. Blend together while adding preferred liquid until desired consistency is reached.

86. Banana-Pear Smoothie

Preparation time: 5 minutes

Cooking time: 0

Ingredients:

2 cups watermelon

2 bananas

Dash of turmeric

Dash of cinnamon

2 pears

Procedures:

1. Prepare ingredients and place into a blender. Blend together while adding preferred liquid until desired consistency is reached.

87. Asparagus-Pear Smoothie

Preparation time: 5 minutes

Cooking time: 0

Ingredients:

3 pears

2 cups grapes

1 cup asparagus (trimmed)

Procedures:

1. Prepare ingredients and place into a blender. Blend together while adding preferred liquid until desired consistency is reached.

88. Blueberry Asparagus-Pear Smoothie

Preparation time: 5 minutes

Cooking time: 0

Ingredients:

2 pears

2 cups blueberries

1 cup asparagus (trimmed)

Procedures:

1. Prepare ingredients and place into a blender. Blend together while adding preferred liquid until desired consistency is reached.

89. Ginger Green Smoothie

Prep Time: 7 minutes

Cooking Time: 0 minutes

Ingredients:

1 cup of frozen mango pieces

1 apple, peeled, and core removed

¼ teaspoon, fresh ginger

30 ml (2 tablespoons) flax seeds

1 kale leave

60 ml (¼ cup) spinach

15 ml (1 tablespoon) lemon juice

250 ml (1 cup) water

Procedures:

1. Place all the ingredients in blender or juicer and pulse until smooth.
2. Serve and enjoy!

90. Calming Coconut Smoothie

Prep Time: 5 minutes

Cooking Time: 0 minutes

Ingredients:

2 cups pineapple

1 tablespoon coconut oil

1 cup kale

1 pinch of cinnamon

Procedures:

1. Prepare ingredients and place into a blender. Blend together while adding preferred liquid until desired consistency is reached.

91. Anti-Inflammatory Smoothie

Prep Time: 6 minutes

Cooking Time: 0 minutes

Ingredients:

2 cups beets
½ cup almonds
2 oranges
Pinch of turmeric

Procedures:

1. Prepare ingredients and place into a blender. Blend together while adding preferred liquid until desired consistency is reached.

92. Berry Anti-Inflammatory Smoothie

Prep Time: 6 minutes

Cooking Time: 0 minutes

Ingredients:

2 cups of beets

½ of crushed almonds

3 cups strawberries

Dash of turmeric

Procedures:

1. Prepare ingredients and place into a blender. Blend together while adding preferred liquid until desired consistency is reached.

93. Beets'n'Nuts Smoothie

Prep Time: 6 minutes

Cooking Time: 0 minutes

Ingredients:

2 cups beets

½ cup crushed almonds

3 mangos

Dash of paprika

Procedures:

1. Prepare ingredients and place into a blender. Blend together while adding preferred liquid until desired consistency is reached.

94. Cauliflangonut Smoothie

Prep Time: 6 minutes

Cooking Time: 0 minutes

Ingredients:

2 cups of beets
1 cup cauliflower
3 mangos
1 tablespoon coconut oil

Procedures:

1. Prepare ingredients and place into a blender. Blend together while adding preferred liquid until desired consistency is reached.

95. Red And White Smoothie

Prep Time: 6 minutes

Cooking Time: 0 minutes

Ingredients:

2 cups beets

1 cup cauliflower

3 cups strawberries

2 tablespoon coconut oil

Procedures:

1. Prepare ingredients and place into a blender. Blend together while adding preferred liquid until desired consistency is reached.

96. Cauliflower Power Smoothie

Prep Time: 6 minutes

Cooking Time: 0 minutes

Ingredients:

2 cups beets

1 cup cauliflower

3 oranges

1 tablespoon coconut oil

Procedures:

1. Prepare ingredients and place into a blender. Blend together while adding preferred liquid until desired consistency is reached.

Specific Carbohydrate Diet Recipes

Basic principle of the SCD:

No food should be ingested that contains carbohydrates other than those found in fruits, honey, properly prepared yogurt, and those vegetables and nuts listed. The nutrients that you need will be provided daily through the SCD diet. These nutrients that would typically be in grains also are in B vitamins, folic acid, iron, calcium, zinc and magnesium.

1. Almond Flour Waffles

Prep Time: 10 minutes

Cooking Time: 15 minutes

Ingredients:

1 cup of almond flour (or other nut flour)

1/4 teaspoon of salt

1/4 teaspoon of baking soda

4 eggs

1 teaspoon of vanilla

2 tablespoons of natural honey (or another legal sweetener)

1/4 teaspoon of cinnamon (optional)

Orange Honey Syrup

½ cup of honey

¼ cup of fresh orange juice

1/8 teaspoon of vanilla extract (optional)

Procedures:

1. Blend all the ingredients together with a fork or whisk.
2. Heat up your waffle iron.
3. Place the dry ingredients in a mixing bowl, and blend with a whisk.
4. Add the wet ingredients to the dry ingredients. Blend all ingredients together
5. Add 1/4 cup of the batter to your waffle iron and close the lid.
6. When the waffle is ready, take it out, and place it on a plate. Next, add your favorite topping (Toppings are optional, you can always eat plain)
7. Seal left-over waffles and store in the refrigerator. Storage can range from refrigeration for a few days, or seal and freeze for a month

2. Baked Eggs in Harissa Spice

Prep Time: 7 minutes

Cooking Time: 10 minutes

Ingredients:

Olive oil – ½ tsp.
Minced red onion – 2 tbsp.
Petite tomatoes – 14.5 oz. can
Prepared Harissa – 2 tbsp.
Eggs – 4 large
Salt and pepper to taste
Fresh chopped parsley or chives – 1 tsp.

Procedures:
1. Heat a large skillet over medium heat.
2. Add the oil and onion and sauté for 2 to 3 minutes, or until golden.
3. Add harissa, tomatoes, and season with salt and pepper.
4. Increase heat to medium-high and simmer for 3 to 4 minutes, or until the liquid reduces a bit.
5. Reduce the heat to medium-low, then add the eggs. Season with salt and pepper and cover.
6. Cook for 5 minutes, or until the top of the eggs are set.
7. Top with chopped parsley or chives.

3. Breakfast Muffins

Prep Time: 10 minutes

Cooking Time: 0 minutes

Ingredients:

Ghee – 3 tbsp.
Frank's red hot sauce – 3 tbsp(***Caution***)
Coconut aminos – 1 tbsp.
Cayenne pepper – 1/8 tsp.
Red bell pepper – ½, diced small
Green onions – 3 (white and green parts, chopped)
Spinach – 2 cups, chopped
Cooked chicken – 1 cup, cubed
Whole eggs – 8
Salt – ½ tsp.
Black pepper – ¼ tsp.

Procedures:

1. Preheat the oven to 350F.
2. Grease the wells of a 12-cup muffin pan.
3. To make the sauce: melt 2 ½ tbsp. ghee in a small saucepan. Whisk in coconut aminos, hot sauce, and cayenne pepper until combined. Remove from heat and set aside.
4. Melt remaining ½ tbsp. ghee in a skillet over medium-high heat. Sauté onion and bell pepper for 5 minutes, or until slightly softened.
5. Turn off heat. Add cooked chicken, spinach and sauce to onions and peppers. Sit to combine.
6. Divide the chicken-vegetable mixture evenly between wells of the muffin pan.
7. Beat egg with salt and pepper in a bowl and pour over vegetable mixture.
8. Bake at 350F until eggs are set, and a toothpick inserted in the middle comes out clean, about 18 to 20 minutes.

4. Legal French Toast

Prep Time: 10 minutes

Cooking Time: 0 minutes

Ingredents:

8 (400g) whole eggs, large whole

3/4 cup Almond milk

1 tbsp (12g) 'swerve' or another sugar equivalent

1 tsp ACV

1/4 cup Coconut flour

1 large dash Salt

1 tsp Vanilla extract

1/4 cup Butter

1/4 cup Butter, fresh whole

1/2 cup Coconut cream

Procedures:

1. Mix together your coconut flour, sugar equivalent (If it's powdered. If it's a liquid, add with the liquids), baking powder and a dash of salt.
2. In a separate bowl, whisk together 4 of the eight eggs. Add only 1/4 cup of the almond milk and your vanilla. Whisk.
3. Add your dry ingredients to your wet ingredients and whisk, while pouring in your melted butter.
4. Grease 12 microwaveable safe containers, which are fairly wide. I used 8 oz ramekins, but you could also use flat bottomed soup bowls, wide coffee mugs, etc. You could even use tall coffee cups and simply cut your muffins in half.
5. Microwave your muffins. For each muffin, add a minute to the microwave. I did 2 batches of 6, with 6 minutes on the timer for each batch. Total: 12 minutes.
6. While your muffins are nuking, in a large and wide mixing bowl, whisk together your remaining 4 eggs, 1/2 cup of almond milk and 1/2 cup of heavy cream.

7. As your muffins come out of the nuker, pop them out of their containers and let them cool for about 1 minute, just long enough to keep them from cooking the egg mixture. When they are cool enough, add them to the egg mixture and allow to sit for a few minutes; flipping them occasionally. They are somewhat fragile, but not too bad. You can fairly easily grab and flip them around. They will absorb the egg mixture.

8. When they have absorbed some of the egg mixtures, heat a large skillet, sauté pan or flat-top griddle over medium-low heat. Add some of your fresh butter and melt it. Everyone has their own method for doing this. So, I'm just going to say ... Fry like fry your muffins like French toast.

5. Banana Muffins

Prep Time: 10 minutes

Cooking Time: 25 minutes

Ingredients:

4 medium eggs, room temperature
3 tablespoons raw clear honey
1 teaspoon vanilla, unsweetened
2 tablespoons coconut oil, softened
½ teaspoon apple cider vinegar
½ cup coconut flour, unsweetened
¼ cup blanched almond flour
½ teaspoon ground cinnamon
1 teaspoon baking soda
½ teaspoon salt
3 overly ripe medium sized bananas
¼ cup milk / coconut milk / almond milk
¼ cup chocolate chips (optional)*

Procedures:
1. Mix all ingredients in a mixing bowl and spoon into greased muffin tin.
2. Bake 350 degrees for 18-24 minutes until golden brown

6. Grain-Free SCD Waffles

Prep Time: 12 mins

Cook Time: 10 mins

Ingredients:

3 eggs

1 cup raw cashews

1/3 cup almond milk (or any non-dairy milk)

3 tablespoons honey or maple syrup

3 tablespoons coconut oil, melted

¼ teaspoon salt

¾ teaspoons baking soda

3 tablespoons coconut flour

Procedures:

1. Preheat your waffle iron.
2. Combine the eggs, cashews, milk, honey, and melted coconut oil in a blender. A high-speed blender isn't necessary (I use a simple Waring blender), although it will make the process easier. Blend until very smooth and creamy. You may need to stop the blender and push the mixture down the sides a few times to get it all to blend really well.
3. Add the salt, baking soda, and coconut flour, then blend again for about a minute until the dry ingredients are incorporated into the wet.
4. If you're iron requires oil, spread a little coconut oil on both sides. Pour the batter into the waffle iron so it just covers the bottom portion of the iron, being careful not to overfill it as these do rise quite a bit and will spill over.
5. Cook the waffles for about a minute, more or less depending on the heat of your waffle iron. If they release easily with a fork when you open the lid, they are probably done.
6. Repeat until the batter has been used up.

7. Breakfast Cereal Grain-Free

Prep Time: 5 mins

Cook Time: 10 mins

Ingredients:

2 cups chopped almonds

2 cups coconut flakes or chips

1 cup pumpkin seeds

1 cup raisins

1.5 cups Almond milk /Coconut milk

Procedures:

1. Mix all ingredients in a large bowl and then store in an airtight container. Serve with either coconut milk or Almond milk poured over and enjoy!

8. Zucchini Frittata Breakfast Muffins

Prep Time: 10 minutes

Cook Time: 15 minutes

Ingredients:

2 tsps olive oil

6 eggs

1 medium red onion

1 medium courgette (zucchini)

2 cloves garlic

100g mature (sharp) cheddar cheese

Salt & pepper

Butter for greasing the muffin tin

Procedures:

1. Dice up the courgette (zucchini) and red onion and crush or slice the garlic cloves.

2. Heat the oil in a pan and fry off the garlic, onion and garlic until they are softened (about 10mins). Season well with salt and pepper.

3. Meanwhile, turn the oven on to 200C and grease a muffin pan with butter.

4. Break the eggs into a bowl, add plenty of salt & pepper and beat with a fork to combine everything.

5. Grate the cheese and add half to the eggs.

6. When the courgette (zucchini) mixture is ready, add it to the eggs and cheese and stir everything to combine.

7. Pour the mixture into the muffin tins and pop into the oven for 10 mins.

8. After 10 mins, remove from the oven, turn on the grill and sprinkle the remaining grated cheese over the top of each muffin.

9. Pop the muffins back under the grill for a few minutes until the cheese is browned and bubbling. Serve.

9. *Cauliflower Bites & Chili*

Prep Time: 15 minutes

Cook Time: 35 minutes

Ingredients:

1 large cauliflower head

2 tablespoons high heat oil

1/4 teaspoon salt

2 teaspoons of ancho chili powder

Procedures:

1. Preheat your oven to 425°F (220°C or gas mark 7) and prepare a baking sheet with parchment paper.
2. Make the ancho chili pepper powder: Heat cast iron skillet on medium for a few minutes. Once hot, place the dried ancho chili in the skillet and shuffle for a few minutes, or until you begin to smell the aroma of it toasting. Then take it out and let cool. Remove the stem and seeds. Grind the remaining pepper in a coffee bean grinder, spice grinder, or food processor until it is has a powder consistency.
3. Chop the cauliflower into bite-size pieces.
4. Add the cauliflower pieces, ancho chili powder, salt, and oil to a large bowl and toss until the cauliflower is well coated.
5. After spreading the cauliflower across the baking sheet, bake for 30 minutes, or until the cauliflower bites are tender and a bit blackened.
6. Serve hot or very warm, with mint yogurt dip and slices of fresh lime.
7. If you don't have an ancho chile, substitute by mixing chili powder and some paprika or smoked paprika.
8. You can eat this with slices of lime and mint yogurt dip:
9. Includes: 1/4 cup of your favorite homemade yogurt, a few mint leave

10. SCD Beef Borritos

Prep Time: 10 minutes

Cook Time: 15 minutes

Ingredients:

4 oz SCD yogurt

1 1/2 tsp ground cumin divided

1 1/2 ground turmeric divided

1 tablespoon olive oil, or coconut oil

1 lb. sirloin beef trips

1 medium white onion thinly sliced

4 carrots cut into matchsticks

1/2 lb. nappa cabbage thinly sliced.

Tortilla's:

Replace flour tortilla with egg crepe.

SCD Crepes

2 large eggs

2 TB cashew butter

2 TB apple cider

a dash of salt

1/8 tsp vanilla extract

a pinch of cinnamon

a pat of butter

Procedures:

1. Beat eggs and mix in cashew butter and apple cider, salt, vanilla, and cinnamon.
2.
   Heat a small non-stick skillet and pour some of the crepe batter into the pan and swirl the pan to form the crepe.

3. Cook about 40 seconds. Flip and cook for another minute.

11. Beef, Eggplant, Celery & Peppers Stew

Prep Time: 10 minutes

Cook Time: 7 hours

Ingredients:

1 cup cubed eggplant
2 cups chopped onions
2 tbsp. coconut oil
1 cup sliced celery
Salt, ground black pepper to taste
1 cup sliced red peppers
4 pounds beef meat cut into stripes

Procedures:

1. Put ingredients in the slow cooker. Cover, and cook on low for 7 to 9 hours.

12. Chicken & Onion Stew

Prep Time: 10 minutes

Cook Time: 7 hours

Ingredients:

1 cup sliced mushrooms
6 large onions, quartered
2 tbsp. coconut oil
Salt, ground black pepper to taste
2 cups chicken stock
4 pounds chicken drumsticks with skin on

Procedures:

1. Put ingredients in the slow cooker. Cover, and cook on low for 7 to 9 hours.

13. *Zucchini Rolls*

Prep Time: 10 minutes

Cook Time: 7 hours

Ingredients:

1 cup brown rice

2 cups chopped onions
2 tbsp. coconut oil

3-4 large zucchinis cut into thick stripes (see picture)

Salt, ground black pepper and ground cumin to taste

2 cups beef stock

4 pounds minced beef meat

Procedures:

1. Mix spices, meat, rice and onion, fill zucchini stripes with the mixture, make rolls and arrange them in the slow cooker. Add beef stock slowly by pouring by the sides. Cover, and cook on low for 7 to 9 hours.

14. Beef Pot Roast with Broccoli

Prep Time: 12 minutes

Cook Time: 7 hours

Ingredients:

2 cups chopped onions
2 tbsp. coconut oil
3 cups broccoli
Salt, ground black pepper & 2 bay leaves
2 cups beef stock
2 tsp. minced garlic
4 pounds beef pot roast

Procedures:

1. Put ingredients in the slow cooker. Cover, and cook on low for 7 to 9 hours.

15. *Mixed Seafood, Saffron & Sundried Tomatoes*

Prep Time: 10 minutes

Cook Time: 7 hours

Ingredients:

1 cup sundried tomatoes

2 cups chopped onions

2 tbsp. coconut oil

1/4 cup olive oil mixed with 1 tsp. saffron

Salt

2 cups white wine

4 pounds frozen mixed seafood

Procedures:

1. Put ingredients in the slow cooker. Cover, and cook on high for 90 minutes.

16. Sloppy Joe Baked Sweet Potatoes

Prep Time: 15 minutes

Cook Time: 6 minutes

Ingredients:
Sweet potatoes – 4 medium, washed and dried (7 oz. each)
Lean ground beef – ½ lb. 93%
Seasoned salt – 1 tsp.
Chopped carrot – 1/3 cup
Chopped onion – 1/3 cup
Chopped mushrooms – 1/3 cup
Chopped red bell pepper – 2 tbsp.
Garlic – 1 clove, minced
Red wine vinegar – ½ tbsp.
Tomato sauce – 8 oz. can
Tomato paste – 2 tsp.
Water – 1/3 cup
Chopped scallion -1, for garnish

Procedures:
1. Poke holes all over the sweet potatoes with a fork. Then cook in an oven or slow cooker until tender.
2. Heat a medium skillet over medium-high heat.
3. Add the meat, season with steak seasoning and cook. Break up the meat into small pieces.
4. Add the onion, red peppers, mushrooms, carrots, and garlic to the skillet.
5. Lower the heat to medium. Then add Worcestershire sauce and red wine vinegar. Cook for 5 minutes.
6. Add water, tomato paste, and sauce to the skillet. Stir to combine.
7. Cover and cook for 15 to 20 minutes, or until carrots are tender.
8. Cut sweet potatoes open, then sprinkle with salt.
9. Top each with ½ cup of meat and garnish with scallion.

17. Cauliflower Soup with Roasted Brussels Sprouts

Prep Time: 7 minutes

Cook Time: 25 minutes

Ingredients:

Cooking spray
Cauliflower florets – 16 oz.
Brussels sprouts – 16 oz. halved
Olive oil – 2 tbsp.
Butter – 1 tsp.
Chopped shallots – ½ cup
Vegetable broth – 3 ½ cups
Kosher salt – ¾ tsp.
Black pepper to taste

Procedures:

10. Preheat the oven to 450F.
11. Line a large baking sheet with foil, then spray with oil.
12. Place the Brussels and cauliflower on the baking sheet (cut side down).
13. Drizzle with oil and roast on the lower part of the oven until slightly browned, about 25 minutes.
14. Meanwhile, in a large saucepan, melt the butter over low heat and add the shallots. Cook for 5 minutes, or until translucent.
15. Add the broth and simmer for 5 minutes.
16. Close the oven door. Set aside about 1 cup of roasted vegetables.
17. Transfer the rest to the pot and simmer for 2 minutes.
18. In a blender, blend until smooth in batches.
19. Serve in 4 bowls top with fresh black pepper and roasted vegetables.

18. *Turkey Taco Lettuce Wraps*

Prep Time: 10 minutes
Cook Time: 25 minutes

Ingredients:

Lean ground turkey – 1.3 lbs. 93%
Garlic powder – 1 tsp.
Cumin – 1 tsp.
Salt – 1 tsp.
Chili powder – 1 tsp.
Paprika – 1 tsp.
Oregano - ½ tsp.
Small onion – ½, minced
Bell pepper – 2 tbsp. minced
Water – ¾ cup
Tomato sauce – 4 oz. can
Iceberg lettuce leaves – 8 large
Shredded reduced fat cheddar – ½ cup, optional

Procedures:

1. In a large skillet, brown turkey and break it into smaller pieces.
2. Once browned, add dry seasoning and mix well.
3. Add tomato sauce, water, onion, pepper, and cover. Simmer for 20 minutes.
4. Divide the meat among 8 leaves and top with cheese.

19. Canned Tuna Ceviche

Prep Time: 10 minutes
Cook Time: 25 minutes

Ingredients:

Minced red onion – 2 tbsp.
Limes – 1 or 2
Kosher salt and black pepper as needed
Olive oil – 1 tsp.
Chunk white albacore tuna packed in water - 1 (7 oz.) can, drained
Seeded plum tomato – 1 medium, finely diced
Chopped cilantro – 2 tbsp.
Jalapeno – 1, minced
Tabasco sauce – 3 drops, optional
Sliced avocado – 2 oz.

Procedures:

1. In a bowl, combine olive oil, juice of 1 lime, a pinch of kosher salt and red onion.
2. Mix in the tabasco, tomato, drained tuna, jalapeno, and chopped cilantro. Taste and adjust seasoning.
3. Cover and marinate in the refrigerator for minimum 20 minutes.
4. Top with fresh sliced avocado and serve.

20. California Grilled Chicken with Vinaigrette Dressing

Prep Time: 10 minutes
Cook Time: 35 minutes

Ingredients:
Grilled chicken breast – 12 oz. (about 1 lb. raw)
Diced avocado – 1 cup
Diced mango – 1 cup
Diced red onion – 2 tbsp.
Baby red butter lettuce – 6 cups
For the vinaigrette:
Olive oil – 2 tbsp.
White balsamic vinegar – 2 tbsp.
Salt and fresh pepper to taste

Procedures:
1. In a bowl, whisk vinaigrette ingredients and set aside.
2. Toss red onion, chicken, mango and avocado together.
3. Divide baby greens into 4 small dishes.
4. Top with avocado-chicken mixture and drizzle half the dressing or top.
5. Serve with the rest of the dressing.

21. Blueberry Chicken Salad

Prep Time: 10 minutes

Cook Time: 35 minutes

Ingredients:

Boneless, skinless chicken breasts – 2 (cooked, cooled and cubed)
Fresh blueberries – ½ cup
Diced celery – ¼ cup
Diced red onion – ¼ cup
Chopped walnuts – 3 tbsp.
Fresh rosemary leaves – 1 tbsp. chopped
Sea salt – ¼ tsp.
Black pepper – 1/8 tsp.
Homemade mayo – ¼ cup

Procedures:

1. To make the salad: in a bowl, combine cooked chicken and remaining ingredients in a bowl.
2. Add mayo and stir to combine.
3. Serve with cucumber slices, or over a bed of mixed greens.

22. Steak Kebabs with Chimichurri

Prep Time: 10 minutes

Cook Time: 10 minutes

Ingredients:

Beef – 1 ¼ pounds (cut into 1-inch cubes)
Fresh ground pepper to taste
Kosher salt – 1 ¼ tsp.
Red onion – 1 large, cut into large chunks
Cherry tomatoes – 18
Bamboo skewers – 6, soaked in water for 1 hour

chimichurri sauce:

Finely chopped parsley – 2 tbsp. packed
Chopped cilantro – 2 tbsp. packed
Red onion – 2 tbsp. finely chopped
Garlic – 1 clove, minced
Extra virgin olive oil – 2 tbsp.
Apple cider vinegar – 2 tbsp.
Water – 1 tbsp.
Kosher salt – ¼ tsp.
Fresh black pepper – 1/8 tsp.
Crushed red pepper flakes – 1/8 tsp.

Procedures:

1. Season the meat with salt and pepper.
2. For the sauce: in a bowl, combine olive oil, salt, vinegar, and red onion and set aside for 5 minutes.
3. Now add the remaining ingredients and keep in the refrigerator until ready to use.
4. Onto the skewers, place the beef, onions, and tomatoes.
5. Prepare the grill on high heat.
6. Grill the steaks 2 to 3 minutes per side for medium-rare.
7. Transfer steaks to a platter and top with chimichurri sauce.

23. *Garlic Shrimp with Tomatoes*

Prep Time: 10 minutes

Cook Time: 20 minutes

Ingredients:

Jumbo shrimp – 1 ¼ lbs. (peeled and deveined)
Extra virgin olive oil – 1 tsp.
Red bell pepper – 1, sliced thin
Thinly sliced scallions – 4, white and green parts separated
Cilantro – ½ cup
Garlic – 4 cloves, minced
Kosher salt to taste
Crushed red pepper flakes – ½ tsp.
Diced tomatoes – 14.5 oz. can
Light coconut milk – 14 oz. can (50% less fat)
Lime – ½, squeezed

Procedures:

1. Heat oil in a medium pot over low heat. Add red peppers and sauté for 4 minutes, or until soft. Add garlic, red pepper flakes ¼ cup cilantro and scallion whites. Cook for 1 minute.
2. Add coconut milk, tomatoes and salt to taste. Cover and simmer on low heat for 10 minutes to thicken the sauce.
3. Add shrimp and cook for 5 minutes. Add lime juice.
4. Divide among 4 bowls and top with cilantro and scallions.

24. Thai Coconut Shrimp Curry

Prep Time: 10 minutes

Cook Time: 20 minutes

Ingredients:

Oil – 1 tsp.
Chopped scallions – 4, whites and greens separated
Thai red curry paste – 1 tbsp.
Garlic – 2 cloves, minced
Shrimp – 1 lb. peeled and deveined
Light coconut milk – 6 oz.
Fish sauce – 2 tsp.
Fresh cilantro – ¼ cup, chopped
Salt to taste

Procedures:

1. Heat oil over medium-high heat in a large skillet.
2. Add scallion whites and curry paste and sauté for 1 minute.
3. Add garlic and shrimp. Season with salt and cook for 2 minutes.
4. Add fish sauce and coconut milk, mix well. Simmer until shrimp is cooked through, about 2 to 3 minutes.
5. Remove from heat; mix in cilantro and scallion greens.
6. Serve over rice.

25. *Spiced Flounder with Tomatoes*

Prep Time: 10 minutes

Cook Time: 20 minutes

Ingredients:
Olive oil – 1 tsp.
Flounder fillets – 4 (6 oz.) pieces
Onion – ¾ cup, chopped
Garlic – 2 cloves, minced
Diced green bell pepper – ¾ cup
Tomatoes – 2 ½ cups, chopped
Cajun spice seasoning – 1 tbsp.

Procedures:

1. In a deep skillet, heat olive oil over medium heat. Cook onion and garlic until soft.
2. Add spices, peppers, and tomatoes. Cook and stir for 2 to 3 minutes, or until tomatoes are soft.
3. Place fillets in the sauce. Cover and cook on medium heat for 12 to 15 minutes, or until fish flakes easily.
4. Place fish on plate and spoon sauce on top.
5. Serve.

26. Beef, Cabbage, and Tomato Soup

Prep Time: 10 minutes

Cook Time: 50 minutes

Ingredients:

Lean ground beef – 1 lb. 90%
Kosher salt – 1-1/2 tsp.
Diced onion – ½ cup
Diced celery – ½ cup
Diced carrot – ½ cup
Diced tomatoes – 28 oz. can
Chopped green cabbage – 5 cups
Homemade beef stock – 4 cups
Bay leaves – 2

Procedures:

1. Heat a large pot over medium-high heat.
2. Spray with oil and add ground beef. Season with salt and pepper and cook for 3 to 4 minutes, or until browned. Break the meat into smaller pieces.
3. When browned, add carrots, celery, and onion and sauté for 5 minutes.
4. Add the bay leaves, beef stock, cabbage, and tomatoes. Cook on low heat for 40 minutes, covered.

27. Cuban Picadillo

Prep Time: 10 minutes

Cook Time: 50 minutes

Ingredients:

Onion – ½ chopped large
Garlic – 2 cloves, minced
Chopped tomato – 1
Pepper – ½, finely chopped
Cilantro – 2 tbsp.
Lean ground beef – 1 -1/2 lb. 93%
Tomato sauce – ½ can (4 oz.)
Kosher salt
Fresh ground pepper
Ground cumin – 1 tsp.
Bay leaf – 1 or 2
Alcaparrado or green olives – 2 tbsp.

Procedures:

1. In a large pan, brown meat on high heat. Break up the meat into smaller pieces and season with salt and pepper. Drain all juice from pan, when meat is no longer pink.
2. Meanwhile, chop cilantro, tomato, pepper, garlic and onion.
3. Add to the meat and continue to cook on low heat.
4. Add alcaparrado, bay leaf, cumin and more salt according to taste.
5. Add ¼ cup of water and tomato sauce and mix well.
6. Lower heat and simmer 20 minutes, covered.

28. *Chicken and Sweet Potato*

Prep Time: 15 minutes

Cook Time: 7 hours

Ingredients:

2 cups cubed sweet potato

2 cups chopped onions

2 tbsp. coconut oil

3 red peppers, chopped

Salt, ground black pepper and ground cumin to taste

2 cups chicken stock

4 pounds chicken meat

Procedures:

1. Put ingredients in the slow cooker. Cover, and cook on low for 7 to 9 hours.

29. Teriyaki Chicken & Carrots

Prep Time: 15 minutes
Cook Time: 7 hours

Ingredients:

2 cups sliced carrots
1 Tbsp. minced ginger & 2 garlic cloves, minced
2 Tbsp. honey
1/4 cup rice or apple cider vinegar
2 tbsp. coconut oil
1 cup onions, chopped
3 Tbsp. fish sauce
1 cup chicken stock & 3 Tbsp. cornstarch (optional)
4 pounds chicken meat

Procedures:

1. Put ingredients in the slow cooker. Cover, and cook on low for 7 to 9 hours.

30. *Spicy Beef Stew –Korean Style*

Prep Time: 15 minutes
Cook Time: 7 hours

Ingredients:

2 cups dried shiitake mushrooms
1 cup chopped onions
4 cloves minced garlic
1 Tbsp. minced ginger
2 cups green onions, cut in half
1 tbsp. sesame oil
2 cups sprouts
2 Tbsp. Fish sauce, hot pepper flakes to taste
2 cups chicken stock
4 pounds beef brisket

Procedures:

1. Put ingredients in the slow cooker. Cover, and cook on low for 7 to 9 hours.

31. Cacciucco - Shrimp, Mussels, Fish & Scallops Stew

Prep Time: 15 minutes
Cook Time: 7 hours

Ingredients:

2 cups tomato paste
2 cups chopped onions
2 tbsp. coconut oil
1 cup cherry tomatoes
Salt, 2 Tbsp. chopped dill.
4 cups fish or vegetable stock
1 pound shrimp
1 pound mussels
1 pound scallops
1 pound local fish

Procedures:

1. Put ingredients in the slow cooker. Cover, and cook on low for 7 to 9 hours.

32. Chicken Stock

Prep Time: 10 minutes
Cook Time: 12 hours

Ingredients:

1 medium {quartered} onion

1 chicken carcass

3 quartered celery stalks

3 quartered carrots

Water to cover the chicken

1 Tablespoon apple cider vinegar

Procedures:

1. Add all of the components for the stock into a slow cooker/crock pot.
2. Strain the final product and freeze or refrigerate. Cook Time: 12 to 18 hours

33. *Sweet Potato Soup*

Prep Time: 20 minutes
Cook Time: 1 hours

Ingredients:

1 diced onion

1 Tablespoon coconut oil

4 C. diced bell peppers {approximately}

2 Cups mashed sweet potatoes

4 Cups chicken stock

Juice of ½ of a lemon

1 teaspoon cumin

1 Tablespoon thyme

Red pepper flakes

To Taste: Pepper and salt

Procedures:
1. Heat the oven ahead of time to 350F. Bake the potatoes for one hour, peel, and throw them into the blender.
2. Using a big soup pot, add the coconut oil, onions, and peppers; sauté until tender.
3. Meanwhile, add two cups of the chicken stock {unheated} with the potatoes and combine until you reach the desired consistency.
4. Combine the puree into the soup and mix well, adding the remainder of the chicken stock. Pour in the lemon juice, thyme, and cumin. Raise the heat bringing the ingredients to a simmer.
5. Garnish with a dollop of coconut cream, red pepper flakes, thyme, pepper, and salt to your liking.

34. *Taco Soup*

Prep Time: 10 minutes
Cook Time: 4 hours

Ingredients:

3 sliced farm-fresh carrots

1 Pound ground beef

2 diced bell peppers

2 to 3 chopped garlic cloves

1 small diced onion

¼ Cup taco seasoning {see below}

3 Cans organic fire-roasted diced tomatoes

Procedures:

1. Combine the garlic with the beef and par-cook it briefly. Add it to the slow cooker with the remainder of the ingredients.
2. Cook on low for four to five hours.

Taco Seasoning for the Soup:

Ingredients:
2 Tbsp. Chili powder
1 tsp. each: Onion powder, Black pepper
, Garlic powder
2 tsp. each: Dried oregano, Cumin, Salt
½ tsp. each:
Paprika
Cayenne pepper
Ground coriander

Procedures for Seasoning:
1. Mix all of the ingredients in a small container.
2. For each pound of ground beef, use approximately 1 ½ tablespoons per pound of the mixture.

35. *Mushroom Burgers*

Prep Time: 10 minutes
Cook Time: 20 minutes

Ingredients:

2 Tablespoons fresh chopped sage

¼ Pound mushrooms

Fresh ground black pepper

3 garlic cloves {pressed}

4 Tbsp. {divided} olive oil

1 Pound lean ground beef

Procedures:

1. Set the oven temperature in advance to 350°F.
2. Wash and chop the mushrooms into quarter sections. Put them in a cookie tin with a rim and bake until they are reduced in size by half, usually for 15 to 20 minutes.
3. Using the medium heat setting, warm up the oil in a pan; blend in the sage and garlic, cooking for about three minutes. Place the mushrooms and the mixture into a processor until they are in small pieces. Add the beef and pulse to combine the burger mix.
4. Make the patties and add the remainder of the oil to the pan; cook for about five minutes per side.

36. Beef Ragu

Prep Time: 15 minutes
Cook Time: 20 minutes

Ingredients:

¼ Cup or 65 g red pesto

1.8 Pounds Ground Beef

1 Tbsp. Butter or ghee

½ tsp. Pink Himalayan salt {more or less}

2 to 4 Tablespoons fresh chopped parsley

Procedures:

1. Put the meat into a hot skillet with the butter/ghee {save some butter for the zoodles}.
2. Cook until it is browned, around five minutes should be sufficient. Toss in the salt, parsley, and pesto; continue cooking about three to five more minutes.
3. When the meat is finished cooking, move it into a dish.
4. Prepare the zoodles: The zoodles are merely four medium zucchini {one per serving}. You make them using a vegetable spiralizer or julienne peeler. Add the inner core to the zoodles.
5. Add the zoodles to the remainder of the components and continue cooking for about two to five minutes.
6. Turn off the heat and serve.

37. Corned Beef in the Slow-Cooker

Prep Time: 10 minutes
Cook Time: 8 hours

Ingredients:

4 carrots
6 red skin potatoes
4 Pounds Corned beef brisket {uncooked}
1 seasoning packet {note}
6 Cups water

Procedures:

1. Combine all of the ingredients into the cooker for eight hours using the high setting.

38. Ground Beef Stir Fry

Prep Time: 10 minutes
Cook Time: 7 minutes

Ingredients:

2 Cups frozen stir fry veggies

1 Pound ground beef

½ cup sliced onions

2 Tablespoons minced garlic

Fresh ground pepper and sea salt to your liking

Procedures:

1. In a medium-sized skillet, brown the beef and add the onions and garlic.
2. After the beef is half cooked, add the veggies and cook for approximately three to five additional minutes.
3. Serve straight out of the pan and garnish as you wish.

39. Marinara Beef Roast

Prep Time: 10 minutes
Cook Time: 10 hours

Ingredients:

2 diced onions

1 teaspoon salt

1 {3-Pound} Beef roast

1 Jar organic marinara sauce

½ teaspoon each:

Fresh ground black pepper, Cayenne

Procedures:

1. Blend all of the ingredients in your slow cooker and relax with the setting on low for ten hours.
2. At that time, you can shred the beef and cook an additional hour with the lid a bit to the side to reduce some of the liquid/steam.

40. Meatballs in a Hurry

Prep Time: 10 minutes
Cook Time: 20 minutes

Ingredients:

1 Pound Grass-fed ground beef, Ground pork
1 teaspoon each: Onion Powder, Sea salt Garlic Powder
2 Tablespoons dried parsley
¾ teaspoon black pepper

Procedures:

1. Set the oven temperature to 400°F.
2. Mix all of the ingredients in a large mixing container.
3. Measure out 1/3 cup portions of the meat and roll into balls.
4. Arrange them on a baking sheet and bake for approximately 15 to 20 minutes.

41. Taco Casserole

Prep Time: 10 minutes
Cook Time: 45 minutes

Ingredients:

2 onions {diced or grated}
2 pounds ground beef {or another type of ground meat}
1 pound each diced or grated: Carrots Potatoes
2 {15-ounce} Cans diced tomatoes
4 Tablespoons chili powder
½ Tablespoon salt
4 Tablespoons cumin
Optional: 1 teaspoon hot sauce

Procedures:

1. Set the oven temperature to 350°F.
2. Use a large pan over med-high heat to prepare the ground beef. Drain it by tilting the pan and scooping out the liquid with a spoon.
3. Cut up/shred the veggies if you have a food processor or grate with a cheese grater.
4. Once the beef is done; add the tomatoes and seasonings. Arrange everything into a rectangular baking dish {9x13 is good}. Bake for 45 minutes.
5. Top it off with some guacamole for a tasty garnish.

42. Venison Burgers

Prep Time: 15 minutes
Cook Time: 15 minutes

Ingredients:

1 Pound ground venison {453.59g}

1 Tablespoon each: Garlic powder Onion powder

½ Cup freshly chopped parsley {118 5/17ml}

To Taste: Pepper and Sea Salt

1 Cup sliced onions {236.59ml}

1 Tablespoon each: Bacon/other cooking fat, Balsamic vinegar

Optional: 1 egg

Procedures:

1. Mix the venison, onion powder, pepper, salt, chopped parsley, and garlic powder in a large mixing container.
2. Shape the meat into four to five patties. The venison tends to have less fat, so you may need to whisk an egg into the mixture to hold it together.
3. Use high heat to melt your choice of fat, add the patties, cover them, and cook three to four minutes per side.
4. When you flip the burgers, add the onions, but watch them closely so they do not burn. Turn down the heat some so that the bits will caramelize.
5. Take the burgers off the heat and set them to the side to drain; add the vinegar to the pan and deglaze to make the 'gravy.' Spoon the gravy over the burgers and serve with a tasty veggie.

43. Chicken Tenders

Prep Time: 10 minutes
Cook Time: 18 minutes

Ingredients:

1 Pound skinless chicken breast cut into strips

½ Cup Almond Meal

¼ teaspoon ground coriander seed

¾ teaspoon paprika

¼ teaspoon ground cumin seed

½ teaspoon salt

1 egg {beaten}

Procedures:

1. Prepare a baking sheet with a layer of parchment paper.
2. Set the oven temperature to 425°F.
3. Mix all of the spices and the almond meal in a shallow container.
4. Break and beat the egg into a separate shallow dish.
5. Use some paper towels to pat the chicken dry. Dip it into the egg first, and then the almond mixture—making sure to coat all of the sides evenly.
6. Bake and turn once about midway of the cooking cycle to ensure even temperature ranges which should be 180°F when the tenders are ready.

44. *Chili Roasted Chicken Thighs*

Prep Time: 5 minutes
Cook Time: 15 minutes

Ingredients:

1 Tbsp. Olive oil

2 Pounds Chicken thighs {boneless}

1 Tbsp. Chili powder

Fresh ground pepper and Sea Salt

Optional: Fresh cilantro for garnish

Lime wedges for serving

Procedures:

1. Heat the oven in advance to 375°F.
2. Arrange the chicken on a baking sheet with a rim.
3. Drizzle it with the oil and give each of the thighs a rub with the pepper, salt, and chili powder.
4. Roast the chicken for about 15 minutes.
5. Sprinkle some of the cilantro on them and serve with a lime wedge or two.

Yields: Four Servings

Prep time: Five min.

Cooking time: Fifteen min.

45. *Indian Style Chicken Drumsticks*

Prep Time: 5 minutes
Cook Time: 40 minutes

Ingredients:

2 to 3 Tbsp. Salt

3 to 4 Tbsp. garam masala

10 Chicken Drumsticks

Procedures:

1. Heat the oven to 450°F.
2. Use some coconut oil to grease a large baking tray.
3. Combine the garam masala and salt in a dish.
4. Dry the drumsticks with a paper towel. Coat them with the mixture and arrange on the prepared tray. Try not to let them touch so that they will cook evenly.
5. Bake for forty minutes.

46. *Sweet Potato and Sausage Casserole*

Prep Time: 15 minutes
Cook Time: 45 minutes

Ingredients:

1 ½ lbs. breakfast sausage

4 cups kale

¼ cup coconut milk

12 eggs, whisked

1 teaspoon pepper

2 sweet potatoes, peeled and diced

1 teaspoon sea salt

½ large sweet onion, diced

¼ teaspoon nutmeg

1 teaspoon garlic powder

Coconut oil

Procedures:

1. Set the oven to 375 degrees. Use coconut oil to grease a 9x13 casserole dish.
2. Grease a skillet with coconut oil and place it over medium heat.
3. Add sausage to the skillet and break it down using a wooden spoon. Cook until brown.
4. Put onions and sweet potatoes together in a food processor and shred. Once done, transfer contents into a large bowl.
5. Add remaining ingredients into the bowl and mix well.
6. Pour the egg mixture into the casserole dish. Add cooked sausage and distribute evenly.
7. Place casserole in the oven and bake for about 45 minutes.
8. Once done, cover the casserole dish with foil and bake for another 10 minutes.

47. *Chicken and Avocado Salad*

Prep Time: 10 minutes
Cook Time: 30 minutes

Ingredients:

4 skinless chicken thighs, deboned

½ red onion, diced

1 teaspoon chili powder

2 small tomatoes, diced

1 teaspoon cumin

1 teaspoon sea salt

3 avocado, peeled and seeded

1 tablespoon avocado oil

Lime juice

Black pepper

Procedures:

1. Set the oven to 350 degrees.
2. Place chicken thighs side-by-side in a glass baking dish.
3. Sprinkle cumin, chili powder, salt and oil on top.
4. Bake chicken for about 30 minutes or until cooked through.
5. Place avocado in a bowl and mash it lightly using a fork.
6. Add onion, chicken and tomato. Drizzle with lime juice and stir well. Season to taste.

48. *Pineapple and Pork Stir-Fry*

Prep Time: 10 minutes
Cook Time: 12 minutes

Ingredients:

1 ½ lbs. pork tenderloin

1 tablespoon tapioca starch

1 large bell pepper, chopped

2 cloves garlic, minced

1 onion, chopped

1-inch piece ginger, minced

20 oz. pineapple

¼ cup pineapple juice

¼ cup coconut aminos

Sea salt

Ghee

Ground black pepper

Procedures:

1. Slice pork and pineapple into chunks.
2. Fry pork in ghee using a skillet for about 5 minutes. Stir continuously.
3. Remove from heat once done and set aside.
4. Place ginger, garlic and onion in the skillet. Sauté for about 2 minutes.
5. Add pineapple and bell pepper. Once slightly tender, pour pineapple juice and coconut aminos into the mixture.
6. Place the pork back in the skillet. Add tapioca starch and stir well to combine.

49. *Fruit Cake*

Prep Time: 5 minutes
Cook Time: 15 minutes

Ingredients:

1 ½ cups almond flour

½ teaspoon sea salt

½ cup tapioca flour

1 cup preferred dry fruits, assorted

½ teaspoon baking powder

1 cup dried cherries

5 eggs

2 cups raisins

1 cup honey, raw

1 cup dates, chopped

1 cup ghee

1 teaspoon vanilla extract

1 teaspoon cloves, ground

1 teaspoon nutmeg, ground

1 teaspoon cinnamon, ground

Procedures:

1. Heat an oven to 350 degrees beforehand. Grease a loaf pan using non-stick cooking spray.
2. Put almond flour, salt, tapioca flour and baking powder in a bowl. Mix well.
3. Add cloves, nutmeg and cinnamon into the mixture. Combine ingredients thoroughly.
4. Whisk eggs, honey, butter and vanilla together in a separate bowl.
5. Combine the two mixtures together. Mix until smooth.
6. Add dried fruits and stir well until evenly distributed.

7. Pour the mixture into the loaf pan and place it in the oven. Cook for about an hour.

50. Raspberry, Watermelon and Mint Salad

Prep Time: 5 minutes
Cook Time: 15 minutes

Ingredients:

½ cup hazelnuts

¼ cup mint, shredded

1/3 cup water

1 ½ cups strawberries, hulled and sliced

¼ cup lime juice

1 cup raspberries

1 tablespoon honey, raw

½ small watermelon

Procedures:

1. Set an oven to 350 degrees.
2. Place the hazelnuts on a baking tray and place it in the oven. Cook for about 10 minutes.
3. Once done, remove the skins from the nuts. Chop coarsely.
4. Combine water, honey and lime juice together in a saucepan. Warm the mixture up over low heat for about 5 minutes then set aside.
5. Remove the rind of the watermelon and discard. Cut flesh into chunks and place these in a bowl together with raspberries, mint and strawberries.
6. Pour liquid mixture over the fruits and mix gently. Garnish with nuts.

51. *Egg in a Jar*

Prep Time: 10 minutes
Cook Time: 35 minutes

Ingredients:

4 large eggs

1 tablespoon ghee

¾ lb. button mushrooms, sliced thinly

2 teaspoons lemon juice

4 slices bacon

½ cup chicken stock

2 green onions, minced

1 teaspoon almond flour

1 tablespoon chives, minced

Ground black pepper

Sea salt

Procedures:

1. Cut bacon into chunks.
2. Using a skillet, cook bacon in ghee over medium-high heat for about 10 minutes.
3. Add green onions and mushrooms to the skillet and cook for another 5 minutes.
4. Add almond flour and mix well. Pour chicken stock together with lemon juice into the mixture.
5. Bring mixture to a boil and cook until smooth.
6. Grease the insides of 4 glass jars using ghee. Transfer equal amounts of the bacon mixture into each jar.
7. Crack an egg on top of each. Season with black pepper and salt.
8. Put the jars into a cooking pot. Pour water into the pot until it covers half of the jars.
9. Place the pot over medium-high heat and cook for about 20 minutes.
10. Remove the jars from the pot once done. Garnish with chives.

52. *Thai Pork Lettuce Wraps*

Prep Time: 10 minutes
Cook Time: 10 minutes

Ingredients:

1 lb. pork, sliced thinly

1 tablespoon ghee

2 cups chicken stock

1 lime, quartered

2 tablespoons white wine vinegar

¾ lb. mung bean sprouts

1 teaspoon sambal sauce

½ cup almond butter

4 tablespoons water

1 tablespoon fish sauce

Fresh lettuce leaves

Ground black pepper

Sea salt

Procedures:

1. Pour chicken stock into a pan. Bring it to a boil over medium-high heat.
2. Add pork and cook gently for about 5 minutes.
3. Once cooked, transfer the pork to a plate and set aside to cool. Pour chicken stock into a separate bowl and refrigerate for later recipes.
4. Grease a pan using ghee. Add bean sprouts and cook for about 4 minutes.
5. Combine all of the remaining ingredients together in a bowl except for lettuce leaves and mix well.
6. Cut lettuce leaves into 3x3-inch pieces. Distribute pork, bean sprouts and almond butter mixture into each leaf.
7. Drizzle with lime juice on top of each and roll into wraps.

53. Stuffed Calamari

Prep Time: 10 minutes
Cook Time: 15 minutes

Ingredients:

4 large calamari

14 oz. tomato puree

5 oz. kale, chopped

1 onion, minced

1 teaspoon dried oregano

1 red bell pepper, chopped

2 tablespoons parsley, chopped finely

2 cloves garlic, minced

Ghee

Ground black pepper

Sea salt

Procedures:

1. Remove the tentacles from the calamari. Chop these finely and set aside.
2. Using a skillet, sauté onions and garlic in ghee over medium heat. Add bell peppers and continue cooking.
3. After 3 minutes, put tentacles in the skillet and cook for another 8 minutes.
4. Add kale and cook until soft. Stir frequently while cooking and remove from heat once done.
5. Divide the mixture into 4 equal amounts and use it to stuff each calamari. Use toothpicks to close up each calamari.
6. Put some ghee in the skillet and place it over medium-high heat.

7. Cook each side of the calamari for about 2 minutes. Add tomato puree together with oregano and parsley. Stir gently and season to taste.
8. Reduce the heat and bring mixture to a simmer. Cover the pan and cook for about 40 minutes.
9. Adjust seasoning if necessary.

54. *Fruit Pudding*

Prep Time: 12 hours
Cook Time: 12 minutes

Ingredients:

1 lb. frozen fruit of choice

5 tablespoons tapioca starch

2 cups orange juice

4 mint leaves

Procedures:

1. Put orange juice and fruits in a saucepan and place it over medium heat. Bring it to a simmer.
2. After a few minutes, use a fine mesh sieve to strain the mixture.
3. Transfer the fruit residue in a separate bowl and place it in the refrigerator.
4. Bring the fruit juice to a simmer. Using a ladle, pour a portion of the fruit juice in a bowl.
5. Add water and tapioca starch into the bowl and mix well.
6. Once combined thoroughly, pour the fruit juice mixture back into the saucepan and stir well until thick.
7. Distribute the mixture evenly into 4 glasses. Refrigerate for at least 2 hours or overnight.
8. Garnish with extra fruit slices and mint leaves.

55. Lemon Chicken Stir Fry

Prep Time: 10 hours
Cook Time: 12 minutes

Ingredients:

1 lemon

1/2 cup chicken broth

3 tbsp. fish sauce

2 teaspoons arrowroot flour

1 tbsp. coconut oil

1 pound boneless, skinless chicken breasts, trimmed and cut into 1-inch pieces

10 ounces mushrooms, halved or quartered

2 cups snow peas, stems and strings removed

1 bunch scallions, cut into 1-inch pieces, white and green parts divided

1 tbsp. chopped garlic

Procedures:

1. Grate 1 tsp. lemon zest. Juice the lemon and mix 3 tbsp. of the juice with broth, fish sauce and arrowroot flour in a small bowl.
2. Heat oil in a skillet over high heat. Add chicken and cook, stirring occasionally, until just cooked through. Transfer to a plate. Add mushrooms to the pan and cook until the mushrooms are tender. Add snow peas, garlic, scallion whites and the lemon zest. Cook, stirring, around 30 seconds. Add the broth to the pan and cook, stirring, 2 to 3 minutes. Add scallion greens and the chicken and any accumulated juices and stir.

56. Pan seared Brussels Sprouts

Prep Time: 10 minutes
Cook Time: 12 minutes

Ingredients:

6 oz. cubed pork

2 tbsp. coconut oil

1 pound Brussels sprouts, halved

1/2 large onion, chopped

Salt and ground black pepper

Procedures:

1. Cook pork in skillet over high heat. Remove to a plate and chop.
2. In the same pan with pork fat, add coconut oil over high heat. Add onions and Brussels sprouts and cook, stirring occasionally, until sprouts are golden brown.
3. Season with salt and pepper, to taste, and put the pork back into the pan.

57. Macadamia Hummus with Vegetables

Prep Time: 20 minutes

Refrigerating Time: 30-45 minutes

Ingredients:

750 ml (3 cups) macadamia nuts
60 ml (¼ cup) freshly squeezed lemon juice
60 ml (¼ cup) olive oil
2 garlic cloves, minced
2.5 ml (½ teaspoon) salt
125 ml (½ cup) water
500 ml (2 cups) of baby carrots
1 English cucumber, shopped into sticks
1 Sweet pepper, deseeded and sliced

Procedures:

1. Place all the ingredients in food processor except carrots and cucumbers and blend until smooth and thick.
2. Place hummus in a bowl and refrigerate to chill for 30 to 45 minutes before serving. Will keep for up to a week in the refrigerator.
3. Serve with the cut vegetables.

58. Beef Goulash

Prep Time: 20 minutes
Cooking Time: 2 hours

Ingredients:

1 kg (2 pounds) boneless stew beef such as chuck roast
30 ml (2 tablespoons) olive oil
1 large onion, chopped
4 garlic clove, minced
5 ml (1 teaspoon) caraway seeds
1 red bell pepper, deseeded, julienne
2 sweet potatoes, peeled and cubed
2 tomatoes, chopped
5 ml (1 teaspoon) salt
15 ml (1 tablespoon) jalapeños pepper, minced
500 ml (2 cups) beef broth
Salt and pepper

Procedures:

1. Cut beef into same size cube, about 4-5 cm (1-2 inches). Dry beef with a paper towel.
2. Heat oil in a large and deep skillet. Add beef, and brown the meat very well, in batches if necessary. For proper browning, the beef cubes should not touch each other in the pan. Remove the meat from the skillet and reserve.
3. Add oil if necessary. Sauté onions for few minutes until translucent. Add in garlic, and cook for 2 minutes. Add the spices, mix well. Add red bell peppers and tomatoes and cook for 5 minutes. Add the reserved beef
4. Season with salt and pepper to taste, and add the jalapeños chili.
5. Add broth, and bring to a boil on high heat. Reduce heat to medium-low. Cover and cook for 1h00. Add sweet potatoes, and cook for an additional 30 minutes. The

meat should be very tender and easily cut with a fork. Taste and adjust seasoning with salt or pepper.

6. Serve hot with a side green salad.

59. Baked Beef with Vegetables

Prep Time: 10 minutes

Marinating Time: 2 hours

Cooking Time: 35 minutes

Ingredients:

30 ml (2 tablespoons) coconut oil

225 g (½ pound) boneless beef strips

1 small red onion, chopped

2 cloves garlic, chopped

125 ml (½ cup) carrots, sliced

1000 ml (4 cups) butternut squash, chopped

1 sweet potato, chopped

2.5 ml (½ teaspoon) dried thyme

2.5 ml (½ teaspoon) dried rosemary

60 ml (¼ cup) coconut amino

2.5 ml (½ teaspoon) ground black pepper

Procedures:

1. In a large bowl, add all ingredients except vegetables. Mix well. Let marinate for 30 minutes.
2. Preheat the oven to 180°C/350° F.
3. Toss in vegetables as well.
4. Place beef and vegetables in the baking dish, cover the dish completely with foil, and bake for 30 to 35 minutes. After that, remove foil, and roast again for 10 minutes.

60. *Quick Chocolate Bonbon*

Prep Time: 20 minutes

Cooking Time: 5-10 minutes

Freezing Time: 20 minutes

Ingredients:

125 ml (½ cup) dark chocolate chunks (70% or more cocoa)

250 ml (1 cup) raspberry, packed (fresh or frozen)

15 ml (1 tablespoon) of raw honey

5 ml (1 teaspoon) crushed almonds

Procedures:
1. Melt chocolate over double boiler. You can also microwave the chocolate until just melted.
2. Take a paint brush, and paint a mini cupcake mold or a candy mold with the chocolate. Paint thickly all around walls and base of the cups, remembering to keep a little melted chocolate for covering the candies.
3. Place in freezer to set for 10 minutes.
4. In the meantime, puree the raspberry in a blender or food processor until smooth, and strain it through a fine sieve to remove the seeds. Add the raw honey to the raspberry puree, and mix well. Set aside
5. After 10 minutes, remove from freezer. Equally spoon the raspberry puree in all the chocolate molds. Sprinkle with crushed almonds. Paint the top with the melted chocolate to cover the bonbons.
6. Place in freezer again to harden for 10 minutes.
7. Lastly, pop the candies out of the mold into a plate, keeping upside down and serve.

61. Cherry and Almond Butter Milkshake

Prep Time: 5 minutes

Cooking Time: 0 minutes

Ingredients:

1cup almond milk

1 whole banana, frozen

8 cherries, frozen

30 ml (2 tablespoons) almond butter

15 ml (1 tablespoon) honey

Ice cubes, as many as you like

Procedures:

1. Place all the ingredients into food processor, and blend until smooth and creamy. Serve and enjoy!

62. Ginger Brownies

Prep Time: 5 minutes

Cooking Time: 25 minutes

Ingredients:

500 ml (2 cups) almond flour

125 ml (½ cup) coconut flour

60 ml (4 tablespoons) cocoa powder, unsweetened

0.5 ml (⅛ teaspoon) cinnamon

Pinch of salt

2 eggs

30 ml (2 tablespoons) coconut oil

30 ml (2 tablespoons) raw honey

15 ml (1 teaspoon) pure vanilla extract

1 teaspoon ground nutmeg

1 ml (¼ teaspoon) fresh ginger, minced

Procedures:

1. Preheat the oven to 200°C/400°F. Lightly grease a baking pan.
2. Mix almond flour, coconut flour, cocoa powder, cinnamon, and salt in a bowl.
3. In another, bowl whisk the eggs.
4. Mix eggs with flour mixture and remaining ingredients.
5. Place in to the baking pan.
6. Bake for 20-25 minutes until a toothpick inserted in the center comes out clean.

63. Watermelon & Kiwi with Fresh Herbs

Prep Time: 10 minutes

Cooking Time: 0 minutes

Ingredients:

1000 ml (4 cups) watermelon

1 kiwi, chopped

2.5 ml (½ teaspoon) fresh oregano, chopped

2.5 ml (½ teaspoon) fresh cilantro, chopped

2.5 ml (½ teaspoon) fresh mint leaves

2.5 ml (½ teaspoon) fresh basil leaves, chopped

2.5 ml (½ teaspoon) fresh parsley, chopped

0.5 ml (⅛ teaspoon) salt

Pinch of ground black pepper

Procedures:

1. Toss all ingredients in a mixing bowl and season with salt and pepper.

64. SCD Beef Borritos

Prep Time: 15 minutes

Cooking Time: 7 minutes

Ingredients:

Beef borritos:

4 oz SCD yogurt

1 1/2 tsp ground cumin divided

1 1/2 ground turmeric divided

1 tablespoon olive oil, or coconut oil

1 lb. sirloin beef trips

1 medium white onion thinly sliced

4 carrots cut into matchsticks

1/2 lb. nappa cabbage thinly sliced.

Tortillas:
Replace flour tortilla with egg crepe.

SCD Crepes

2 large eggs

2 TB cashew butter

2 TB apple cider

a dash of salt

1/8 tsp vanilla extract

a pinch of cinnamon

a pat of butter

Procedures:

1. Beat eggs and mix in cashew butter and apple cider, salt, vanilla, and cinnamon.
2. Heat a small non-stick skillet and pour some of the crepe batter into the pan and swirl the pan to form the crepe.
3. Cook about 40 seconds. Flip and cook for another minute.
4. Assemble burrito!

65. *Roasted Tomatoes*

Prep Time: 10 minutes

Cooking Time: 5 Hours

Ingredients:

Pre -heat oven to 225*F.
Roma Tomatoes cut in half

Chopped Garlic...

Fresh Rosemary, Thyme Fresh Oregano is my Fav

Pinch of salt and pepper

Procedures:

1. Drizzle with coconut or olive oil
2. Bake/Roast on cookie sheet 5-6 hours.
3. Sprinkle with parmesan.

66. *Specific Carbohydrate Diet Guacamole*

Prep Time: 10 minutes

Cooking Time: 0 Hours

Ingredients:

Cool Guacamole

4 ripe avocado

Juice of ½ lemon or lime

1 teaspoon salt

1/2 teaspoon ground cumin

1/2 teaspoon granulated garlic

1/4 teaspoon coriander

1/4 teaspoon pepper (or to taste)

1/4 teaspoon cayenne or chili powder (optional)

1 tablespoon chopped cilantro (optional)

1 medium tomato finely chopped (optional)

Procedures:

1. Slice the avocado and place in a bowl.
2. Add the remaining ingredients and smash with a fork or spoon. Mix well but leave "chunky"

67. Pulled Hawaiian Pork

Prep Time: 10 minutes

Cooking Time: 5 Hours

Ingredients:

Pulled Pork 250*F. oven

1 three lb pork loin

1/2 cup Soy Sauce

1/2 cup apple cider

Fresh Thyme Herbs

1 Can Diced Pineapple

Procedures:

1. Place meat in roasting pan and coat with all ingredients.
2. Cook the roast 5 hours or until pork pulls apart with a fork.

68. SCD Shrimp Scampi

Prep Time: 5 minutes

Cooking Time: 10 Minutes

Ingredients:

1lb of shrimp with olive oil

Garlic 2-3 cloves

Cherry tomatoes halved

1/2 cup SCD legal vegetable broth.

2-3 T butter

Fresh oregano thyme tarragon

Juice of lemon or lime

Procedures:

1. In a pan on medium high heat, add oil, melt butter and ad juice of lemon or lime, herbs and garlic.
2. Let cook 1-2 minutes then add shrimp.
3. Cook 3-4 minutes until shrimp or bright red.
4. Do not overcook.

69. Eggs Baked in Avocado

Prep Time: 5 minutes

Cooking Time: 10 Minutes

Ingredients:

1 avocado

2 eggs

4-5 cherry tomatoes

1-2 garlic cloves,

Fresh cilantro

Salt and pepper

Procedures:

1. Cut the avocado in half, and scoop out more than the pit, just enough to hold a hardboiled egg.
2. Crack each egg into each avocado half and place on a cookie sheet or baking dish.
3. Top with chopped tomatoes all seasoning and herbs
4. Bake for 20 minutes or until eggs are cooked.

70. Awesome Blossom Cauliflower

Prep Time: 5 minutes

Cooking Time: 20 Minutes

Ingredients:

1 large head of Cauliflower cut into pieces

6-8 strips of bacon cooked and chopped or pancetta cubed

6 tablespoons chopped Chives and fresh dill

2 cups Colby Jack Cheese (or Romano)

2-3T olive oil

Procedures:

1. Place Cauliflower on a baking sheet and drizzle with olive oil spices herbs and cheese.
2. Bake for 15-20 minutes @ 425 Degrees until cheese is melted.
3. Top with remaining 3 T chives and serve.

71. *Bacon Wrapped Steak with Onions and Mushrooms*

Prep Time: 5 minutes

Cooking Time: 12 Minutes

Ingredients:

2 fillet mignon medallions

8 oz whole mushrooms, sliced in half

1 medium onion, sliced

8-10 slices bacon*

2 tbs olive oil

1 tsp salt

1/2 tsp pepper

Procedures:

1. Wrap bacon around fillets, season with salt and pepper and place on the bbq grill.

2. Sauté onions and mushrooms pour over steak.

72. *Roasted Brussels Sprouts in Avocado Oil with Orange and Pomegranate*

Prep Time: 7 minutes

Cooking Time: 45 Minutes

Ingredients:

1/4 Cup Extra-Virgin Avocado Oil

Juice and Zest of 1 Orange

1 Tablespoon Honey

1/2 Teaspoon Sea Salt (ground)

1/2 Teaspoon Pepper

2 Pounds Fresh Brussels Sprouts (cored)

1/2 Cup Pomegranate Arils

Coarse Sea Salt

Procedures:

1. Preheat oven to 400°F.
2. Whisk the oil, orange juice, zest, honey, and salt and pepper in a large bowl until well combined. Add the Brussels sprouts to the mix (leave them whole or halve them for quicker cooking time) and toss to coat.
3. Lay on a baking sheet in a single layer, being careful not to overcrowd. Roast until the sprouts start to tenderize and turn brown, about 40-50 minutes. Remove from oven and toss with the pomegranate seeds and a sprinkling of coarse sea salt.

73. *Thai Style Carrot Soup*

Prep Time: 10 minutes

Cooking Time: 25 Minutes

Ingredients:

2 tablespoons olive oil, coconut oil, or ghee

1 large onion, diced

About 1 inch slice of fresh ginger, peeled and grated (about 1 teaspoon)

1 1/2 teaspoon curry powder

1/2 teaspoon salt

3 to 4 cups broth or water

2 pounds carrots, peeled and chopped into coins

1/4 cup coconut milk (or other milk)

1 to 2 tablespoons of fresh lemon juice (optional)

Procedures:

1. Place a stock pot over a medium heat.
2. Once the pot is warmed, add the oil.
3. Add the onions and cook for 5 to 10 minutes, or until they're becoming translucent.
4. Add the spices and salt to the onions, and stir to coat them evenly.
5. Add the stock or water, and the carrots.
6. Bring the soup to a boil and then simmer for 15 minutes or until carrots are tender throughout.
7. Add coconut milk and stir until blended well.
8. Optionally, add the lemon juice and stir to blend well.
9. Blend the soup with a blender stick, or do it in batches using a blender. If you do it in batches let it cool first for a bit. I leave my soup a bit lumpy, but you can blend it until it's completely smooth too.
10. Serve with goat cheese, lemon yogurt, pesto, roasted cauliflower rice, or just have it plain.

74. Peanut Butter Cookies

Prep Time: 5 minutes

Cooking Time: 12 Minutes

Ingredients:

1/2 cup raw clear honey*...[substitute for 1 cup sugar which is not legal]

1 cup peanut butter*

1 egg

Procedures:

1. Mix all ingredients.
2. Roll into balls on silpat or cookie sheet.
3. Press with a fork.
4. Bake 8-10 minutes. 375*F oven temp
5. Take out of oven and sprinkle with coconut (unsweetened)

75. SCD Legal Sandwich Bread

Prep Time: 5 minutes

Cooking Time: 12 Minutes

Ingredients:

1 cup smooth raw cashew butter at room temperature

4 large eggs, separated (mine weighed about 9 ounces in their shells)

½ to 2 tablespoons honey (use 2tbl if you plan to use if for sweeter dishes like French toast)

2.5 teaspoons apple cider vinegar

¼ cup almond milk

¼ cup coconut flour

1 teaspoon baking soda

½ teaspoon sea salt

Procedures:

1. Preheat your oven to 300 degrees. For a white colored loaf as in the photo, place a small dish of water on the bottom rack.

2. Line the bottom of an 8.5×4.5 glass loaf pan with parchment paper, then spread a very thin coating of coconut oil on the sides of the pan.

3. Beat the cashew butter with the egg yolks, then add the honey, vinegar, and milk. I've done this with both electric hand beaters and a stand mixer and both seem to work equally as well. I would not try to make this by hand due to the stickiness of the butter.

4. Beat the egg whites in a separate bowl until peaks form. I used an electric hand mixer, but if you want a bicep workout, you can also do it by hand.

5. Combine the dry ingredients in another small bowl. Sorry for all of the dishes!

6. Make sure your oven is completely preheated before adding the egg whites and the dry ingredients to the cashew butter mixture. You don't want your whites to fall, and the baking soda will activate once it hits the eggs and vinegar.

7. Pour the dry ingredients into the wet ingredients, and beat until combined. This will result in more of a wet batter than a dough. Make sure to get all of the sticky butter mixture off of the bottom of the bowl so you don't end up with clumps.

8. Pour the beaten egg whites into the cashew butter mixture, beating again until just combined. You don't have to be gentle with this, but don't over mix.

9. Pour the batter into the prepared loaf pan, then immediately put it into the oven.

10. Bake for 45-50 minutes, until the top is golden brown and a toothpick comes out clean. Don't be tempted to open the oven door any time before 40 minutes, as this will allow the steam to escape and you will not get a properly risen loaf.

11. Remove from the oven, then let cool for 15-20 minutes. Use a knife to free the sides from the loaf pan, then flip it upside down and release the loaf onto a cooling rack. Cool right-side up for an hour before serving.

12. Wrap the loaf up tightly and store in the fridge for 1 week. I actually think the loaf gets better as the days go on.

Conclusion

I hope this book has given you some new ideas for recipes and that you have found some favorites. As you have learned, the human body evolved to naturally digest fruits, vegetables, meats and fish over thousands of years. And finally, there is a diet that can truly supply the human body with what it was meant to ingest.

The next step is to make the recipes included in this book, utilizing them to fuel your gut healing, better overall health and energy. Take what you love about them and keep it. If you hated the recipe try taking out one ingredient and adding in another. I know not every recipe or smoothie will be to your liking, but that is what makes the variety of over 170 recipes so great. There is so much flexibility.

Eat good food drink healthy smoothies to a better healthier you.

Please feel free to look into the author's other books related to curing Ulcerative Colitis and Crohn's disease that works in conjunction with these recipes

How To Cure Ulcerative Colitis In 90 Days: Alternative Non-Toxic Treatment That Works Kindle Edition
https://www.amazon.com/dp/B06VTKPTKV

How To Cure Crohn's Disease in 90 Days: Alternative Healthy Treatment That Works Kindle Edition https://www.amazon.com/dp/B06XKNC3NT

Made in the USA
Columbia, SC
25 May 2023

17301339R00124